QUALITATIVE
DISASTER RESEARCH

D1610449

SERIES IN UNDERSTANDING STATISTICS

S.NATASHA BERETVAS   Series Editor

SERIES IN UNDERSTANDING MEASUREMENT

S.NATASHA BERETVAS   Series Editor

SERIES IN UNDERSTANDING QUALITATIVE RESEARCH

PATRICIA LEAVY   Series Editor

Understanding Statistics

Exploratory Factor Analysis
Leandre R. Fabrigar and
Duane T. Wegener

Validity and Validation
Catherine S. Taylor

Understanding Measurement

Item Response Theory
Christine DeMars

Reliability
Patrick Meyer

Understanding Qualitative Research

Oral History
Patricia Leavy

Fundamentals of Qualitative Research
Johnny Saldaña

The Internet
Christine Hine

Duoethnography
Richard D. Sawyer and Joe Norris

Qualitative Interviewing
Svend Brinkmann

BRENDA D. PHILLIPS

QUALITATIVE
DISASTER RESEARCH

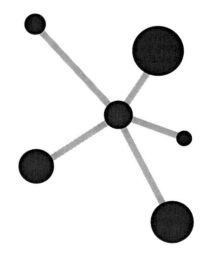

OXFORD
UNIVERSITY PRESS

OXFORD

UNIVERSITY PRESS

Oxford University Press is a department of the University of Oxford.
It furthers the University's objective of excellence in research, scholarship,
and education by publishing worldwide.

Oxford   New York
Auckland   Cape Town   Dar es Salaam   Hong Kong   Karachi
Kuala Lumpur   Madrid   Melbourne   Mexico City   Nairobi
New Delhi   Shanghai   Taipei   Toronto

With offices in
Argentina   Austria   Brazil   Chile   Czech Republic   France   Greece
Guatemala   Hungary   Italy   Japan   Poland   Portugal   Singapore
South Korea   Switzerland   Thailand   Turkey   Ukraine   Vietnam

Oxford is a registered trademark of Oxford University Press
in the UK and certain other countries.

Published in the United States of America by
Oxford University Press
198 Madison Avenue, New York, NY 10016

© Oxford University Press 2014

Library of Congress Cataloging-in-Publication Data
Phillips, Brenda D.
Qualitative disaster research / Brenda D. Phillips.
    pages cm
Includes bibliographical references and index.
ISBN 978-0-19-979617-5 (pbk. : alk. paper)   1. Disasters—Research.
2. Disaster relief—Research.   3. Qualitative research.   I. Title.
HV553.P525 2014
363.34072′1—dc23
2013043002

Dedicated to
E.L. Quarantelli and David M. Neal

CONTENTS

ACKNOWLEDGMENTS

I want to thank Patricia Leavy (series editor) and Abby Gross (Oxford University Press) for recognizing a need for a book on qualitative disaster research methods. Though methods of studying disasters and catastrophes do not vary from other social sciences, the context does. Conducting research on an event yet to happen can be challenging as researchers do not know where, when, or who they might study. In the aftermath of an event, entering and gathering rich and relevant data can be complicated, including entering affected areas to find displaced people amidst disrupted places.

Writing such a volume rests on the efforts of others, particularly those who originated the area of disaster studies. I am indebted to E.L. Quarantelli, a student of the "Chicago School" and co-founder of the Disaster Research Center (DRC). Professor Quarantelli saw potential in a new graduate student sitting in his classroom several decades ago. At the end of that class, he offered me a position as a graduate research assistant at DRC, where I learned first-hand how to enter the field, gather and analyze data, and write up the findings. I am humbled by the investment of time Professor Quarantelli and other mentors have given me, which compels me to do the same today in my own classes and through this book.

While at the DRC, I met a fellow graduate student researcher who became my research collaborator and life partner. I am grateful to Dave Neal for believing in me as well and for his abilities to always see the larger picture theoretically and empirically. I dedicate this volume to Professors Quarantelli and Neal.

Other mentors have influenced my work as well. Dr. Laurel Richardson patiently discussed many aspects of writing, from the placement of quotes to the presentation of self, and others. Dr. Robert Stallings (a DRC alum and fellow Buckeye) invited me to write a chapter on qualitative disaster research which first appeared in the Volume 15/1 issue of the *International Journal of Mass Emergencies and Disasters* and later in his edited volume *Methods of Disaster Research*. Dr. Dennis Wenger provided important mentoring while serving as director of the Hazards Reduction and Recovery Center at Texas A&M University. He gave valuable guidance on how to present one's work positively when seeking external funding. I am especially thankful for the support of disaster colleagues over the years who published their own work, shared their wisdom on qualitative methods, and always said kind words about my own. I especially thank Pam Jenkins, Eve Coles, Maureen Fordham, Elaine Enarson, and Lori Peek.

This volume reflects the work of important scholars, many of whom are recognized as exemplars throughout the coming chapters. This intentionally short book could never capture the contributions of many other scholars whose qualitative disaster research deserves recognition. To write this volume, I erred on the side of choosing classic pieces. I also tried to select works that reflected interests from other nations. I offer my sincere apologies to anyone who may have felt left out in this focused volume. Please believe in yourself and your work.

Finally, I am particularly appreciative of my parents, Frank and Mary Jane Phillips, who supported me from graduate school to this day. To help complete this volume, they generously provided "doggie day care" so that I could write. They are truly the best parents on the planet.

QUALITATIVE
DISASTER RESEARCH

1

INTRODUCTION

DISASTER RESEARCH, as an area of inquiry, has openly embraced publishing qualitative studies—far more so than many other specializations or disciplines. Historically, much of early disaster research developed out of qualitative research designs. Prince (1920) first studied disasters after an explosion in Halifax, Canada. Other critical studies followed, particularly those that emanated from traditions in hazards research, the "Disaster Research School," and risk management (Mileti et al. 1995). Today, a long tradition of qualitative studies forms an impressive body of knowledge from discipline-specific and interdisciplinary scholars.

Researchers conceptualize key terms (hazards, risk, disasters) in qualitative disaster research differently (Cutter 2002). The term *hazard* represents a threat to people and places. Using systems theory, a hazard threatens society when human systems, the built environment, and physical conditions interact poorly (Mileti 1999). For example, an earthquake (physical system) can "pancake" floors in a building (built environment). People (human systems) become vulnerable to hazards for various reasons. Income, for example, can purchase a safer location in a building retrofitted for an earthquake hazard. Or, people who live paycheck to paycheck may find they cannot afford security from area hazards and, not surprisingly, experience property damage, injuries, or even death. *Risk* can be assessed (often quantitatively and in terms of probability) to determine the likelihood that a hazard will take place (Cutter 2002). When systems fail, sufficient disruption to society can result in a disaster. Most researchers conceptualize a *disaster* as an event that disrupts normal routines—businesses and schools close, hospitals struggle to deliver aid, transportation systems fail, and families cannot care for their kin (see the upcoming section titled "What is a Disaster" for additional details).

A well-established tradition of qualitative disaster research (QDR) continues into the present day, linked to major disaster research centers and notable scholars worldwide. Collectively and independently, disaster researchers rely on qualitative procedures that produce rich insights into how people, organizations, and communities face unanticipated events. Scholars have produced a considerable body of knowledge from efforts that spread across multiple disciplines and may involve collaborative research teams.

Why Qualitative Disaster Research?

Quantitative approaches rely on carefully crafted ways to measure variables. Traditionally, quantitative studies unfold through a deductive approach well-grounded in extant literature, such as commonly occurs in surveys. The difficult-to-anticipate nature of sudden onset disasters means that traditional, time-consuming quantitative studies may not be feasible. QDR stands in contrast to quantitative methods, though both provide valid ways to study disasters. Imagine, for example, trying to deploy a telephone or online survey in an area that now lacks telephone, cell, or Internet service. Furthermore, residents and organizations may have experienced residential displacement. If they were able to return home, they now face daunting clean-up with little time to answer the phone or go online. In some events, such as Hurricane Katrina in 2005 or the Haiti earthquake of 2010, many residents never returned home. Telephone and even door-to-door surveys would have failed, as surveyors would have been hard-pressed to find anyone home.

Disasters also present often-unique configurations of events, processes, and interactions that may not be conducive to traditional, deductive studies. Initially, the 2011 earthquake off the coast of Japan seemed limited to a severe shaking. As soon became clear, tsunami waters rushed inland, claiming tens of thousands of lives. Associated damage caused major failures at the Fukushima nuclear plant. Thousands of people, displaced from their homes, searched frantically for loved ones. Government organizations and volunteers responded in horrific conditions, with private sector workers putting their lives on the line to save others from the nuclear plant situation. Few studies have ever investigated such complex emergencies, let alone the "Na-Tech" (natural-technological) disaster combination found here.

To investigate the complex and rapidly changing environment found in such events requires a more open-ended type of inquiry characterized by inductive approaches (see Table 1.1). Deductive studies that would have relied on existing literature on volunteerism before the 1995 Kobe, Japan earthquake, might have assumed minimal volunteer response. Researchers would have developed surveys based on a presumed lack of volunteer response (due in part to an absence of relevant literature). Yet Kobe emerges as the "renaissance" moment of volunteerism in Japan (Comfort 1996; Tatsuki 1998; Shaw and Goda 2004). An inductive strategy, characteristic of qualitative approaches, would have been flexible enough to assess such altruistic convergence.

New types of disasters also prompt flexible research designs. The social effects of space weather disasters, for example, remain unexamined. However, should a powerful geomagnetic storm disrupt power grids, researchers can anticipate research on related effects for hospitals, assisted living facilities, and home-bound individuals. By designing an inductive approach that directs researchers to create explanations from the data (rather than deductively based hypothesis-testing), it is possible to capture, analyze and report on social phenomena surrounding unanticipated events.

Indeed, what differentiates qualitative disaster research (QDR) from more general qualitative studies is the *context,* particularly in the emergency response time period. Two factors prove critical to successful studies: timing one's arrival on a disaster site and gaining access (Stallings 2006). Navigating through such circumstances demands flexible research designs and creative researchers able to gain entrée and gather meaningful data. Indeed, the goals of qualitative research and QDR remain the same: to collect a detailed data set that reveals the lived experiences of actors and organizations in dynamic social settings (Lofland et al.

Table 1.1
Inductive and Deductive Approaches to Research

Inductive	**Deductive**
Holistic	*Reductionistic, Atomistic*
Looks at the meanings produced by social actors through social interactions, that the "whole is more than the sum of its parts." Example: how do people interpret warning messages prior to taking action?	Focuses on the relationships between variables; on the "parts." Example: which variables predict evacuation behavior?
Understands the broader context rather than specific acts. Example: looks at the constraints on people's choices made by policy, public officials, failure to provide evacuation resources.	Studies acts produced by social actors to explain behavior. Example: which variables predict evacuation behavior?
Interpretive by understanding behavior relevant to the setting. Example: people may rely on social networks to provide shelter or may think that public shelters remain inaccessible or unsafe.	Predictive rather than interpretive. Example: Given the demographic composition of a community (e.g., income, gender, age), approximately 20% will evacuate to a public shelter.
Purposive, sets human behavior in context. Example: people remain in their homes to safeguard their pets and livestock.	Causation is the focus: which specific variables predict who will evacuate with their pets?
Not deterministic.	Deterministic.
Non-standardized techniques, emergent, flexible.	Standardized techniques with set rules for developing and testing hypotheses stating relationship between variables.

Source: Based in part on Quarantelli, circa 1981.

2006). Toward that end, disasters represent a location in which to observe the human condition at a most sincere level of performance (Goffman 1959, 1963) and during which disasters reveal social problems along with the resiliency found in social networks and social structures (Barton 1970). Being witness to such social behavior demands clear and rigorous scientific methodology coupled with a sound understanding of disaster studies. This volume aims to inspire readers toward both.

About This Volume

To understand the use of qualitative methods for disaster research, this chapter defines disasters and then outlines the general areas or "phases" into which most qualitative disaster research falls. A brief history of qualitative disaster studies then follows along with a discussion of factors that have driven the field forward. The chapter concludes by considering what kind of person is well-suited to becoming a qualitative disaster researcher. Subsequent chapters reveal general approaches, specific techniques, and issues associated with qualitative disaster research. Throughout, examples drawn primarily from the disaster research tradition inform the content and provide readers with a guide to understanding, presenting, and critiquing QDR. Classic studies and fresh examples present strategies for how qualitative disaster researchers can report their findings.

For decades, scholars have generated significant research findings through qualitative disaster research designs. They have done so through publishing in well-respected journals and via high-level agencies including the U.S. National Academies of Science and the United Kingdom's Government Cabinet Office. Studies have produced insights into socio-behavioral, community, organizational, governmental, and transnational response in times of crisis. Such a unique combination of basic and applied research has created a body of knowledge exceptionally valuable for academic purposes and society. Qualitative disaster research has clearly generated valuable conceptual and theoretical insights and promulgated useful applications for disaster practice and policy. Furthermore, as *use-inspired research* (Stokes 1997), findings apply beyond disaster contexts. People seeking to understand or manage other crisis occasions such as mass shootings, power outages, and even economic downturns benefit from QDR findings. This volume invites you to learn about that legacy and to participate as a fellow researcher.

What Is a Disaster?

Solid research begins with understanding how researchers conceptually define the main topic under investigation. Researchers have spent decades debating the term "disaster," generating multiple volumes and articles addressing subtleties of varying perspectives on the term (Quarantelli 1998; Perry and Quarantelli 2005; Perry 2006). Scholars debate conceptual definitions for several reasons. First, clear conceptualizations permit greater comparison of events. Second, conceptual clarity helps to move forward a scientific body of knowledge. Despite lingering debates over conceptual definitions, most scholars seem to agree that disasters fall along a continuum from an emergency to a disaster to a catastrophe. *Emergencies* tend to be relatively routine events that occur daily in many communities. In such situations, first responders assist those affected by structural fires, car accidents, or crimes. We may not even notice the emergency if our daily routine did not cross the site where the emergency occurred. Conversely, *disasters* disrupt our routines. Disasters close businesses and schools, displace families, and disturb normal, everyday events like traveling, caring for family, or securing health care. Disasters require more extensive responses than just first responders, and involve a wider range of people, agencies, and organizations, including emergency managers and volunteer organizations. Disasters may require involvement from supportive units outside of the affected area when locals become overwhelmed, including state, regional or national assistance. Further along the continuum, *catastrophes* interrupt such external capacities to help those affected (Quarantelli 2006). The 2010 Haiti earthquake, for example, required assistance from Haitians as well as dozens of other nations and non-governmental organizations (NGOs). Even in the United States (which has extensive crisis resources), hurricane Katrina damaged an area along the Gulf Coast the size of the United Kingdom. Beleaguered governmental agencies and NGOs struggled over where to start and sought resources from across the entire nation. Other nations contributed funds and resources to help those affected. Understanding the differences between these terms serves as an initial point to understand the magnitude, scope, and scale that one's research will address. For example, one would study different organizations in an emergency (fire, police, ambulance) than in a disaster (the same, along with emergency managers, public officials, and NGOs) and then in a catastrophe (regional, national, transnational, and non-governmental actors). The area of the study would vary, too, from focused on an accident at an intersection to many miles or kilometers of affected area. Conceptualizing the start point focuses inquiry and bounds the study, making it manageable to conduct research and allowing others to compare their findings to yours.

Four Phases of Disaster Research

Most disaster research can be organized into four phases: preparedness/planning, response, recovery, and mitigation (National Governor's Association 1979; see Figure 1.1). The bulk of published qualitative disaster research occurs in the preparedness and response phases (Mileti 1999). Several factors have spurred research in these phases, particularly the magnitude of the disaster event and the amount of funding available to conduct studies.

Preparedness (and planning). Preparedness research focuses on household, organization, private sector, and governmental efforts to be ready for disaster. Preparedness might include planning, training, drills and exercises, public education, and building a disaster kit. Quantitative studies tend to dominate

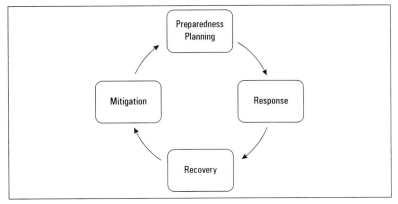

Figure 1.1 The Four Phases of Emergency Management (National Governor's Association 1979)

preparedness and planning, such as efforts that document how many people have a preparedness kit for an earthquake or tornado. We know that individuals, households, organizations, and businesses remain under-prepared, seeing disaster preparedness as a low priority event (Tierney et al. 2009; Mileti 1999). Yet diligent attention to preparedness, often through qualitative methodology, has uncovered reasons why some populations do not prepare. For example, the cost involved in developing a preparedness kit precludes doing so for low-income households, including single parents, some people with disabilities, many seniors, and historically marginalized racial, religious, and ethnic minorities, and households with pets (Irvine 2004, 2006, 2009; National Council on Disability 2010; Phillips et al. 2010; Peek 2011). Further, maintaining preparedness can be challenging (Diekman et al. 2007).

In terms of *planning*, qualitative studies have uncovered that planning is a process requiring stakeholder involvement rather than consultant-delivered boilerplates (Quarantelli 1997). Actors involved in implementing the plan must *know* the plan. Such an outcome occurs when people participate actively in designing the plan, followed by collective training and drilling to learn the plan. The payoff occurs when a disaster begins and the solid relationships established through stakeholder-driven planning generate more effective response.

Response occurs when a disaster is underway, involving people and agencies in sheltering, search and rescue, and efforts to prevent property damage. Funding agencies tend to release grants when major events happen, such as the Japanese tsunami of 2011, the Haiti earthquake of 2010, or Hurricane Katrina in 2005. The bulk of disaster grants fund response time research, sending investigators into the field to gather perishable data on dimensions such as warnings, evacuations, search and rescue, crisis management, infrastructure/utility disruptions, or shelter operations (e.g., see Nigg et al. 2006). The University of Colorado's Natural Hazards Center in the United States funds such Quick Response Studies, with hundreds of reports available on their website (see www.colorado.edu/hazards). Michaels (2003, p. 15) notes: "the intent of quick response research is to understand circumstances that exist only fleetingly and/or to document evidence created as a result of a damaging event that will not survive clean-up operations."

Capturing disaster-time data necessitates rapid entry into affected areas before the phenomena under investigation ends, before those involved in the events disperse, or before data disappears forever (such as information written on erasable boards or search and rescue teams that quickly enter and exit). To overcome challenges associated with such rapid entry, researchers may pre-design research projects, secure funding, and wait for a suitable event to occur (Stallings 2006; Michaels 2003). Qualitative research, though, offers more flexibility in research design which permits studies to emerge and grow as events unfold, a process that will be addressed throughout this volume. Doing so allows researchers to identify and address newly appearing problems that require evidence-based solutions. For example, qualitative studies have assessed the conditions that give rise to emergent citizen groups and volunteer organizations that try to address unmet needs (Stallings and Quarantelli 1985; Neal 1990; Enarson and Morrow 1997).

Recovery, the time period that follows response and includes reconstruction and rebuilding efforts, represents the least-investigated area of inquiry (Mileti 1999) despite the reality that such studies could help people displaced for years and the organizations that try to assist them (e.g., see Weber and Peek 2012). Why? Recovery studies unfold longitudinally, over time, which requires dedicated staffing and funding. Securing the funding and maintaining a research team over 1, 5, or even 10 years can be time-consuming and expensive. Yet, understanding how people move through a recovery process or the factors that improve organizational efficacy would contribute significantly to existing literature and reduce human suffering. Numerous elements of recovery bear further investigation from a qualitative approach: recovery planning, debris management, historical and cultural preservation, "green" rebuilding, business recovery, housing repairs and rebuilding, infrastructure reconstruction, volunteer management, psychological and spiritual recovery needs.

The *mitigation* phase focuses on structural or built efforts (dams, levees) to reduce risk along with non-structural measures as well such as insurance, writing and monitoring building codes, and conducting mitigation planning. The mitigation phase remains under-investigated as well, though in this area structural engineers (sometimes working with social scientists) have made great strides in designing buildings resistant to earthquakes, tornadoes, or terrorist attack. The National Science Foundation in the United States has allocated funds to establish major centers toward this end, including the Pacific Earthquake Engineering Research Center (http://peer.berkeley.edu/). Mitigation researchers using qualitative methods have also investigated how communities and government enact policies to protect people (Olson, Olson, and Gawronski 1998), relocations (Perry and Lindell 1997; Phillips, Stukes, Jenkins 2012), and participatory mitigation planning (Fordham 1999).

A Brief History of Qualitative Disaster Research

The International Research Committee on Disasters (IRCD), which formed in 1982, annually honors a deserving graduate student with the Samuel Prince Dissertation Award. Prince earned recognition as the first person to complete a systematic study of disasters, on a 1917 explosion in Halifax, Canada (Prince 1920; Scanlon 2002). He focused on the social consequences of a collision between two sea-going vessels, one of which carried wartime munitions. The explosion claimed the lives of 1,963 people. Imagine—losing 22% of the community's population in one massive accident. Prince conducted research longitudinally for over two years, documenting and analyzing social change in the aftermath of the disastrous event. To gather data, Prince used three main data sources: interviews, documents, and observation. Subsequent scholars have lauded a "study [that] was grounded in the value of scientific method in developing knowledge to guide future disaster relief efforts in a more rational way" (Quarantelli and Dynes 1992, no page).

To date, the winners of the Prince Award have conducted inquiries in this spirit:

> The Samuel H. Prince Award for a Doctoral Dissertation on a Disaster Topic in the Social and Behavioral Sciences. It is given in recognition for initial and notable accomplishments by disaster researchers in the social and behavioral sciences. The intent in giving this award is to encourage the early identification of exceptional research talent, to the extent it can be indicated by a doctoral dissertation. A committee of five disaster researchers appointed by the IRCD President review nominations for this award and select a final winner. It can be given every year.

As of 2012, three students have earned the coveted Prince Dissertation Award. Dr. Amy Christianson (Ph.D. in Geography, University of Alberta, Canada) used interviews and focus groups to study wildfire risk perception and mitigation Canadian Aboriginal communities. Dr. Bethany Brown (Ph.D. in Sociology, University of Delaware, United States) merited the award for a study examining how domestic violence shelters responded and recovered after two major hurricanes. Dr. Ronél Ferreira (Ph.D. in Educational Psychology, University of Pretoria, South Africa) looked at how an informal settlement community used asset-based resources to cope with HIV and AIDS.

The next forward push of disaster research came in the 1950s, again in the United States. With the Cold War underway, government agencies wanted to know how people, communities, and organizations might respond under attack. Disasters proved to be a comparable ground for conducting applied research on the topic. Assuming first that social disorganization would ensue, government sponsors sought insight into the presumably disruptive influences of panic, looting, disaster shock, and other assumed behavioral responses to war and disaster. Studies, heavily qualitative, proved these assumptions erroneous. The University of Chicago's National Opinion Research Center (NORC) led a series of field studies on a range of events, looking at socio-behavioral responses to social impacts. The National Academy of Sciences also contributed efforts that produced insights into warnings, convergence, organizational response, and more (e.g., see Fritz and Mathewson 1957a; Disaster Research Group 1961; Quarantelli 1987a; Quarantelli 1998). Early efforts such as these produced a group of scholars interested in careers in QDR. As they began to develop their research agendas, they also produced the world's first research centers. Through conducting collaborative research and training their own graduate students, faculty members involved in research centers built a cadre of social scientists firmly grounded in qualitative methodology.

The Rise of Research Centers

In 1962, E.L. Quarantelli, Russell R. Dynes, and Eugene G. Haas co-founded the Disaster Research Center at The Ohio State University. The first of its kind in the world, The Disaster Research

Center (DRC, now at the University of Delaware, visit www. udel.edu/DRC) valued a field based, qualitative research methodology. Such an approach reflected Quarantelli's experience as a graduate student at the University of Chicago. While there, Quarantelli studied under Herbert Blumer, whose methodology and intellectual heritage came from the "Chicago School." In the dynamic urban environment of 1920s Chicago, with new immigrants arriving regularly, researchers at the University of Chicago sent students into the field. Faculty and practitioners conducting studies in the area believed firmly that you had to be in the field to truly understand social behavior (Deegan 1990; Fine 1995). Such an intimate involvement with people often viewed abstractly as "human subjects" provided social and cultural contexts around how people interacted, created and maintained social relationships, and managed daily living. Seeing people in their natural environment fostered rich, deep insights that yielded some of the best empirical work and theoretical insights yet seen in the social sciences.

During the 1960s, the Disaster Research Center followed the Chicago School tradition and sent students into the field. The decade coincided with the publication of key works in a new qualitative analysis approach called grounded theory. Glaser and Strauss (1967) explained how they generated an inductively-based explanation in their book *Discovery of Grounded Theory*. For graduate students associated with DRC, coupling Chicago-style field work with grounded theory resulted in hundreds of publications and reports on disasters, riots, and other forms of collective behavior. In particular, DRC studies (heavily qualitative) disproved a popular social disorganization assumption about about how people and organizations faced crisis and instead empirically induced the reverse. From DRC, we learned that pro-social behavior heavily outweighed antisocial behavior in the response period, that an ability to improvise served crisis managers better than a command and control approach, and that recovery was best conceptualized as a process than as an end goal (for a list of publications, visit www.udel.edu/DRC). Over the last 50 years, the DRC has mentored dozens of graduate students on to careers at the National Science Foundation and the National Academies of Science and as directors at national laboratories and research centers and as practitioners. Their efforts did not stop at U.S. borders.

In 1982, DRC faculty led efforts that launched the International Research Committee on Disasters (IRCD, see http://www. udel.edu/DRC/IRCD.html), also known as Research Committee #39 within the International Sociological Association. The IRCD created the first disaster journal named the *International Journal of Mass Emergencies and Disasters*, which has published many landmark studies using qualitative methods. The IRCD makes back issues prior to the last three years publicly available at their website (visit www.ijmed.org). Scholars present their research annually at IRCD-sponsored conferences in the United States and at the International Sociological Association which meets every four years.

DRC is not the only such center or set of faculty to embrace qualitative approaches. Scholars associated with Florida International University's International Hurricane Center produced a hallmark piece of research after Hurricane Andrew struck Miami and south Dade County in 1992 (Peacock, Morrow, and Gladwin 1997). Qualitative pieces in the volume captured differential social effects of disaster for single mothers, life in tent cities, and the role of urban ecological networks on minority community recovery. Walter Peacock then went on to serve as director of the Hazards Reduction and Recovery Center (HRRC) at Texas A&M University (originally founded by Dr. Dennis Wenger, a DRC alumnus). Well-crafted, signature quantitative and qualitative studies emerged from HRRC, with faculty members spanning sociology, planning, psychology, and other disciplines.

Social scientists in other universities and nations have launched similar efforts. The Natural Hazards Research and Applications Information Center (NHRAIC) at the University of Colorado has produced an impressive and extensive list of field studies conducted as "Quick Response" studies. The NHRAIC began in 1976 under the direction of geographer Gilbert White. Known world-wide as the "father of natural hazard mitigation," White concentrated on mitigation efforts that concurrently maintained ecological integrity (Hinshaw 2006). Under the direction of geographers and sociologists, NHRAIC had funded and published 230 quick response studies by 2012, on topics including warnings, evacuation, and sheltering; impacts on vulnerable populations including children, elderly, and pets; and subjects as diverse as volunteerism, mass fatality management, psychological response, recovery and political turmoil. With support from an array of funders (e.g., the U.S. National Science Foundation), the NHRAIC has provided funding sufficient to send researchers worldwide into areas affected by natural and technological disasters and terrorism. The NHRAIC supports an annual Natural Hazards Workshop near Boulder, Colorado, which brings researchers and practitioners together to build professional networks and transfer use-inspired research (Stokes 1997). The IRCD sponsors a "Researcher Add-On" conference that follows the NHRAIC workshop.

Researchers from the hazards, risk, and fire/wildfire traditions have also produced qualitative studies, centers, and generations of researchers determined to understand the impacts of crisis occasions on people and places. Dr. Susan Cutter, a geographer at the University of South Carolina, directs the Hazards and Vulnerability Research Institute. With funding from the National Science Foundation, NASA, NOAA, and the U.S. Army Corps of Engineers (among others), Cutter and her associates have led efforts in understanding both vulnerability and resiliency from quantitative and qualitative approaches including geographic information systems (e.g., see National Academies 2012).

A number of other centers have evolved over time. At Middlesex University in the United Kingdom, an interdisciplinary effort concentrates researchers on flood disasters. Investigators from geography, environmental sciences, economics, sociology and anthropology examine interactions between people and the environment. Recent studies have focused on capacity building in both the United Kingdom and other nations such as Bangladesh. Work at the Flood Hazard Research Centre also addresses public participation, community resilience, and coastal safety.

Wildfire researchers have recently begun to collaborate and band together in efforts to accumulate studies and foster new efforts. In Australia, the Bushfire Cooperative Research Centre involves social science researchers in both quantitative and qualitative studies (http://www.bushfirecrc.com/). Principal scientific advisors for the Bushfire Cooperative Research Centre include experts at the Royal Melbourne Institute of Technology's Centre for Risk and Community Safety who study community education, economic costs, personal protection strategies, and shared responsibility policies (e.g., Whittaker and Handmer

2010). At the University of Tasmania, investigators study community safety and education (Paton et al. 2008). The University of Melbourne provides social and environmental researchers within their Department of Forest and Ecosystem Science. Others at Central Queensland University examine operational aspects of bushfire suppression. A full list of academic centers can be found at http://www.colorado.edu/hazards/resources/centers/academic.html (last accessed January 2013).

Students from the DRC, TAMU, the NHRAIC, centers in Australia, India, the United Kingdom, Germany, France, and other locales have gone on to produce qualitative studies as the second and third "generations" of disaster scholars. David Neal, a Quarantelli protégé, launched the Center for the Study of Disasters and Extreme Events at Oklahoma State University. Henry W. Fischer, a graduate of the DRC, established the Center for Disaster Research and Education (CDRE) at Millersville University of Pennsylvania. Lori Peek, one of Mileti's mentees, became the co-director of the Center for Disaster and Risk Analysis at Colorado State University. Others have gone into practice, such as Sarah Norman-Black (a student of Dr. Eve Coles from the U.K. University of Leeds), to the New Zealand Ministry of Civil Defence and Emergency Management. In summary, a dedicated core of qualitative researchers, centers, and mentors have driven forward the specialty of QDR across time and around the world. They have taken the body of knowledge produced by many contributors (too many to single out in this volume) and used it to generate theory, to enrich conceptual understanding, to inform evidence-based best practices, and to develop effective policies. The body of knowledge has grown exponentially and rapidly, with periodic assessments that inventory significant numbers of qualitative studies.

Assessing Disaster Research

Jeanette Rayner (in the U.S. National Academies of Science) first offered an annotated bibliography of disasters and "other extreme situations" in 1957. Fritz and Williams (1957) and Fritz and Mathewson (1957a) followed by describing the findings emanating from research to date. The National Academies, which supported work by Fritz and colleagues indicated that they would publish another inventory as soon as needed—which they did a mere two years later in 1961. In this work, the Disaster Research Group (1961, p. 2) described the inventoried field work as "a study in which the behavioral scientist goes to or near the site of any actual or potential disaster, selects some aspect or problem of human behavior in the event and attempts to exercise at least minimal scientific control over the collection, analysis, and reporting processes." The new inventory totaled 114 events in 103 disasters and wartime events including bombings. A total of 21,624 people participated in qualitative interviews or answered questionnaires. The Disaster Research Group at the National Academies, established and working between 1952 and 1962, spurred others onward, saying (1961, p. viii): "the storehouse of our information must be augmented with many rigorous studies. The need should be met by imaginative field studies, as well as experimental ones, with fresh conceptual approaches." DRC became the repository of the Disaster Research Group's work.

Mileti, Drabek, and Haas (1975) produced one of the more frequently recognized efforts, assessing only behavioral science studies of disaster. Nonetheless, they produced a volume of 167 pages. By 1986, Thomas Drabek had published another and more systematic "inventory" of findings dependent on both qualitative and quantitative studies. Drabek organized the 509 page volume into sections on planning, warning, evacuation and other pre-impact mobilization, post-impact emergency actions, restoration, reconstruction, hazard perceptions, and attitudes toward the adoption of adjustments. During the 1990s, Dennis Mileti, a mentee of Gilbert White, convened 100+ experts (academics and practitioners) for a "Second Assessment" of disaster studies. The effort produced seminal volumes that described knowledge to date and served to push forward additional efforts, with all being published by the National Academies (e.g., see Mileti 1999; Burby 1998; Kunreuther and Roth 1998; Tierney et al. 2001; Cutter 2002).

Additional Drivers for Qualitative Disaster Research

Other supporters and drivers of qualitative disaster research have included the development of academic journals, efforts like the

Gender and Disaster Network, the "Enabling Project" sponsored by the U.S. National Science Foundation, and the emergence of disaster studies degree programs.

Journals Dedicated to Disaster Research

QDR scholars have published in discipline-specific journals as well as those dedicated to disseminating disaster studies. In 1975, a first journal dedicated exclusively to disasters appeared. Titled *Mass Emergencies,* the periodical published for a few years as a precursor to the *International Journal of Mass Emergencies and Disasters.* Today, the collective field boasts numerous academic journals. Though studies include quantitative and mixed-methods approaches, disaster-centered inquiry continues to be heavily influenced by qualitative methods. A selective review of several journals substantiates this observation. For example, the six most recent journals available between 2010 and 2012 showed that:

- 71% (12 of 17) of all articles in the *International Journal of Mass Emergencies and Disasters* covered topics qualitatively spanning relocations, popular culture, coping strategies, policies, preparedness, social media, recovery, gender, and domestic violence.
- 70% (7 of 10) of all articles in *Environmental Hazards* presented qualitative studies on community engagement, undocumented workers, participatory risk assessment, recovery, risk intervention, and relocation.
- 45.5% (15 of 33) of all articles in *Disasters* covered research on psychological health, evacuation, risk reduction, behavioral reactions, inequalities, children, social vulnerability, agriculture, ethnicity and social networks, immunizations, preparedness, social vulnerability, relocations, and risk communication.

The Gender and Disaster Network

The Gender and Disaster Network, established in 1997, began initially to encourage understanding around how gender can impact disaster consequences. The Gender and Disaster Network (GDN), first inspired by Mary Fran Myers (co-director of the NHRAIC), met to form mutual ties across nations. Now an international presence, the GDN provides resources, publications, and networks to scholars and practitioners alike. Those mentored within the network have established scholarships and awards to recognize the value of gendered disaster studies, the majority of which require qualitative investigation.

For example, quantitative evidence clearly indicates that female mortality rates are higher in tsunamis, epidemics, and droughts, especially in developing nations (e.g., see OXFAM, n.d.). Qualitative research has dug into these quantitative rates to uncover explanations. A lack of inclusiveness in planning for emergencies has meant that local organizations do not always consider women's perspectives, with clear implications for life safety, property loss, and the burdens of recovery (Enarson and Morrow 1997; Toscani 1998; Fordham and Ketteridge 1998; Fothergill 2004). After the Indian Ocean tsunami, researchers explained that gendered, culturally-appropriate clothing entangled women trying to survive the waves as they waited on the beach to clean and market fish—the men who were in boats at sea survived. Beyond the response phase, qualitative researchers have found that disasters expose female and juvenile survivors to human trafficking and interpersonal violence (Fisher 2005, 2009). During Hurricane Katrina in the U.S., evacuations for women and children staying in domestic violence shelters occurred through the heroic efforts of shelter providers (Jenkins and Phillips 2008). When Katrina inundated huge swaths of the U.S. Gulf Coast, displacing one million people, some women could only regain housing with an abuser. Other women, who shared child custody with an ex-husband on weekends, had to go to court to retrieve their children. From pre- through post-impacts and into long-term recovery, scholars have produced qualitative insights that disasters are not equal opportunity events.

Gendered research has gone on to explore disproportionate ways in which men experience disasters, too. Indeed, gender-segregated workplaces lead to higher rates of death and injuries, such as found within the predominantly-male first responder profession (Phillips and Jenkins 2010). With 96% of the U.S. firefighters being male, the majority of those who died in the attacks on September 11th were male. For Hurricane Katrina, higher death rates among older

African American men (Sharkey 2007) were likely related to the intersection of social class (a lack of evacuation resources) and social isolation (a consequence of gendered family interaction patterns).

The "Enabling Project" in the United States

Sparked by discussion that much could be lost should the disaster, hazards, and risk traditions dwindle across time, key leaders launched efforts to support and mentor the "next generation." What would happen should those who established the first research centers retire? In the United States, the National Science Foundation funded several rounds of mentors and mentees. Known as the "Enabling Project," the effort focused on pairing experienced disaster scholars with academics fresh out of Ph.D. work. Convening at regular intervals over several years (first in 1996 and again from 2002 to 2004), "Enabling Fellows" learned grant writing, theories, and methods from more established investigators.

The effort produced an impressive set of outcomes:

As of late 2007, the two groups of fellows—27 in all—have produced over 42 peer reviewed articles, three books, 22 book chapters in the hazards and disasters field, and were awarded 18 research grants totaling over $3.2 million. Most of the enabling fellows from the first two rounds have continued successful careers in their disciplines and in hazards and disasters studies; many of these fellows are assuming leadership roles in their disciplines and in the research field, and several of the mentors in this year's program are former fellows. (Source: http://www.ncsu.edu/project/nextgen/overview.htm, last accessed January 2013).

From the enabling project, the worldwide set of research centers, the GDN, and similar efforts it is clear that mentoring has produced multiple generations of scholars dedicated to disaster research. Their scholarship, as use-inspired science, has gone into a number of degree programs, thus leveraging an effort spanning multiple generations to produce an expansive body of knowledge.

Programs in Disaster Studies

Collectively, researchers associated with centers and as individuals have supported the evolution of an entirely new discipline, the practice of disaster management. The body of knowledge that informs academic degree programs rises from an array of social sciences including sociology, geography, psychology, political science, economics, social work, disability studies, and even more fields.

In the United States, the Federal Emergency Management Agency (FEMA, http://training.fema.gov/EMIWeb/edu/) and Fire Emergency Services Higher Education (FESHE, http://www.usfa.fema.gov/nfa/higher_ed/) have led efforts to support degree program development in disaster/emergency management, homeland security, fire administration, and related areas. Students may now pursue undergraduate minors or majors, master's degrees, and doctoral degrees. The first such program began at the University of North Texas in the 1980s with an undergraduate bachelor's degree. Since then, FEMA has identified over 200 programs in the United States and abroad, including the United Kingdom, New Zealand, India, Mexico, Canada, Costa Rica, Nepal, Turkey, Australia, and many more nations. Such rapid progress rarely occurs within academic contexts, suggesting that students and prospective employers find value in degree programs. Increasingly, these degree programs include faculty associated with the research centers and programs discussed in this chapter. They dedicate their efforts not only to graduating practitioners but also to researchers as well. If you are one of them, welcome to our field!

Who Should Conduct Qualitative Disaster Research?

Disaster scholars must be particularly well-suited for qualitative field studies or must develop their abilities to do so. Gaining entrée to disaster sites, particularly during the response phase, requires careful negotiation—this is especially true where issues of homeland security exist. Although gaining entrée to disaster sites used to be much easier in the 1970s, 1980s and 1990s, concerns over security of first responders, the privacy of traumatized people living in temporary shelters, and the convergence of unwanted spectators have caused emergency personnel to limit access to potential field research sites.

Although we usually cannot see disasters coming in advance (such as a flash flood or tornado), we can anticipate "seasons" when disasters grow more likely and develop research protocol to apply when opportunities appear. Researchers must be ready to go into "firehouse research" (out the door with a digital recorder in hand) and sufficiently flexible to adapt any research design to any setting. September 11th is a good example. Few researchers could have anticipated the type, intensity, and location of the attacks in 2001. Yet, with funding through the NHRAIC's Quick Response program and other funders, numerous academics made their way to New York, Pennsylvania, and Washington D.C. They studied myriad topics, primarily from a field-based, qualitative stance: victim management (Simpson and Stehr 2003); volunteer behavior (Lowe and Fothergill 2003); group solidarity (Peek 2003); and business response (McEntire, Robinson, and Weber 2003). They put their personal and professional lives on hold to gather information potentially useful in future attacks.

Being open and flexible is not enough to become a good disaster researcher though. QDR requires a particular type of person to conduct qualitative fieldwork. In general, qualitative researchers must be sociable, accepting, and nonjudgmental. They must be truly attentive to what others have to say and understand they need to do *less* talking and *more* listening. Good qualitative researchers remain curious, coupled with a willingness to follow threads of conversation. As one example, investigators must listen for key words, phrases or meanings offered by interviewees that provide subjective insight into their lives, perspectives, and actions. Noting the critical dimension requires deep sensitivity on the part of scholars.

Paying close attention to the nonverbal behavior of the respondent, along with vocal inflections and verbal signals, produces critical insights. As one example, I was interviewing a Mississippian after Hurricane Katrina. When asking about cross-cultural interactions between predominantly white volunteers and a largely African American community, one respondent remarked: "people here remember the swimming pool." Alerted by the words describing an event that occurred in the 1960s, I queried the respondent. He explained that Mennonites had been in the area then to work on issues of social justice—and had built the first pool open to African Americans in a context of deep segregation. By saying that residents remembered the pool, the respondent was signaling that a legacy of standing up for people muted concern over issues of cross-racial interaction then and now.

Fieldwork demands both mental and physical rigor (Plotkin 1993). In the response phase, researchers may need to pack in their own food and water, wear heavy duty boots, and prepare for muck, stench, and potentially hazardous conditions. To capture data during a crisis demands that you must be there, *in the moment*. Leave the field setting and you could miss a critical incident or decision. Simultaneously, you must record and reflect so as not to miss that *critical* moment—and being so completely attentive can be both stressful and exhausting. Long days will unfold that deplete even the most physically fit. After leaving the field, researchers must write up their notes immediately to reduce data loss. For those observing emergency operations, spending 12 hours at the Emergency Operating Center then means 3 to 4 hours writing up notes in a car, coffee shop, truck stop, or (hopefully) an open hotel.

Our Oklahoma State University Hurricane Katrina field team, dispersed across Texas, Louisiana and Mississippi, often drove hundreds of miles every day to reach the next shelter. Yet, after Katrina, the displacement of nearly one million people from the Gulf Coast meant that hotel rooms remained unavailable. We called upon our friends along the coast—who called upon their friends—who offered beds and floor space in private homes. Our eight-person team stayed in the homes of complete strangers connected through casual university ties, often arriving late at night and leaving early in the morning. Even in the midst of personal chaos and loss, fellow academics took us in, taught us about local cultures and communities, and became writing colleagues, and then friends. They saw value in qualitative research as a way to generate meaning from the storm and produce knowledge that would help others in future disasters (Phillips et al. 2012).

Personal qualities are not the only important characteristics to consider. Ascribed statuses, the ones we are born with, often influence our lives and our access to sites, interviewees, and even organizations (Baca Zinn 1979; Townsend-Bell 2009). In his research on the Suriname Indians, Plotkin wrote that "I am convinced that there exists a wealth of ethno-botanical treatments for menstrual problems, birth control, difficult childbirth, and so on, which is simply unavailable to the male ethno-botanist." The same may well be true in disaster studies where issues of gender, race, class, and occupation may influence access, acceptance in a field setting, and what respondents choose to share. It may not be a coincidence that the vast majority of research on domestic violence in disasters has been completed by women.

The notion of the "insider-outsider" is particularly relevant here (Baca Zinn 1979). Gender segregation, for example, means that many first responder and emergency management occupations have been male-dominated. The field of emergency management has historically been dominated by retired military, a characteristic that seemingly increased post September 11th. Fire departments in particular carry reputations of being a closed "brotherhood." Similar to many organizations, firefighters have their own jargon and insider relationships—a highly functional means to build trusted connections between those who face considerable daily risk. The tightness of the firefighter community means that it may be tough to get inside and truly understand how fire services operate. Because the profession has been male-dominated (at present under 4% of all firefighters in the United States are women) and predominantly white (approximately 3% of all firefighters are members of minority groups), it has been difficult for women and minorities to break in to the field. Presumably, the same would be true of a researcher, although Carol Chetkovich (1997) managed to gain unusual access to fire departments in Oakland, California. When the city issued a policy increasing the acceptance of women and minorities, Chetkovich interviewed the new recruits and conducted on-site observations. Despite not being a firefighter, she published a meaningful account of how new recruits became professionals, particularly those facing hurdles based on gender and race.

Similarly, Lori Peek (2011) interviewed Muslim-Americans after 9/11. As a graduate student herself, she found common ground with many respondents attending New York universities. Her work generated significant insights into the pain endured by Muslim-Americans who, often visibly identifiable through cultural and religious practices, became targets of violence. Peek revealed how Muslim-Americans lost the right to mourn the tragedies of 9/11 along with fellow Americans and found themselves cast as symbolic enemies. Enduring hate crimes and exclusionary practices, they developed coping strategies and social networks that enabled them to survive.

Should only insiders conduct disaster research? Though some may argue that only insiders really "get it" about their culture, context, and lived experiences, the rich, perceptive research demonstrated by Chetkovich and Peek suggests otherwise. At the heart of the argument is the ultimate goal of QDR: the emic, or insider perspective. A broader observation is that most research on any topic is conducted by outsiders such as studies on HIV/AIDS, poverty, botany, or animals—so it can be done. There is value, though in developing collaborative field teams to overcome anticipated barriers and to move forward the research effort. When studying the 2004 Indian Ocean Tsunami in India, for example, we hired Oklahoma State University graduate students from India as full team members. Their input provided invaluable guidance on cultural practice and local social, political, geographic, and environmental contexts. The insider-outsider collaboration produced a highly-functional team that generated insights on emergent search and rescue practices and into mass fatality management (Hyrapiet 2006; Phillips et al. 2008).

To summarize, Drabek (2002) advises students of disaster studies to "follow your dreams" and accept opportunities presented to you. The insider-outsider debate matters, but you can move into organizations, agencies, and communities and gather meaningful data. The research centers, studies, publications and practical work described in this volume is proof.

Summary and Looking Ahead

This chapter has provided a general overview of the history and value of qualitative disaster research and the context in which researchers conduct their work. Despite obstacles, studies have revealed critical insights into a wide array of individual, household, organizational, and community experiences into disasters. Qualitative studies have produced an extensive and rich set of findings that reveal the subjective, lived experience of disasters before, during and after they occur. Researchers, often working in arduous conditions, have dedicated themselves to generating understanding through interviews, archival research, visual studies, and observations. Their work, as a form of use-inspired research, has challenged and transformed disaster management and produced valuable conceptual and theoretical insights. You are invited to join these rich qualitative traditions in disaster, hazards, fire, and risk research.

Chapter 2 describes QDR research design. Chapter sections address quick response research and longitudinal designs as well as site selection, entrée, personal safety, and ethical concerns. Standards for the conduct of interviews, observation, unobtrusive measures, and visual research will be illustrated within a disaster context. Chapter 3 lays out a methodology section from initial design through project completion. Topics include sampling, data-collection methods, and data analysis methods. Chapter 4 addresses how to write up research findings. The data reduction process of coding, memo-writing, and analytic strategies will be explained and illustrated with disaster examples. Chapter 5 then explains procedures to evaluate qualitative disaster research. Chapter 6 includes references and additional readings.

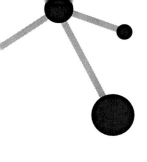

2

RESEARCH DESIGN

Overview of the Chapter

Chapter 2 provides extensive coverage of traditional social science methods for qualitative studies. The chapter begins by discussing commonly used paradigms that organize how researchers approach their work. This section is followed by discussion of ethical concerns both generally and specifically for QDR. Sampling techniques, and the challenges associated with QDR sampling, follow. Discussion of four main methods then ensues: interviewing (including focus groups), observation, unobtrusive measures, and visual research. Each section includes examples drawn from qualitative disaster research as well as citations to specific studies that use the method(s).

Paradigms for Qualitative Disaster Research

As described in Chapter 1, researchers need to think carefully about the way in which they approach their study. Competing paradigms exist to do so, and qualitative research typically stands in contrast to the long-established approach known as positivism.

The positivist model, historically tied to quantitative studies, assumes that "social reality is predictable and can potentially be controlled" (Hesse-Biber and Leavy 2013, p. 8).

In contrast, naturalistic approaches (see Lincoln and Guba 1985) which is also called constructivism (see Erlandson et al. 1993) hold to the idea that social reality needs to be understood in a more complex and nuanced manner. Further, naturalistic approaches call for an emergent research design that frees the researcher to adapt the study as it unfolds. Of particular importance, naturalistic inquiry focuses on the *context* in which a study occurs. For disaster researchers, the context also distinguishes their investigations—one that requires a more flexible approach given the often dynamic nature of events in a disaster, a wildfire, or a terrorist attack. QDR often demands and benefits from a more flexible approach than that mandated by a traditional, quantitative, deductive, and positivist framework.

Lincoln and Guba elaborated on the alternative paradigm of naturalism. Guba (in Erlandson et al. 1993, p. XI) states that researchers bring positivist "baggage" with them including the "lingering effects of ingrained conventional presuppositions." Guba encourages researchers to rethink how traditional science teaches us to approach research. For a naturalistic researcher, findings result from the "hermeneutic-dialectic interaction" between the researcher(s) and study participant(s). Experts recommend that data be produced through a conversational "relationship" that emerges during the interview. To do so, the interviewer and interviewee work collectively to produce useful information (Rubin and Rubin 2012). Guba (1993, p. xiii) concurs, stating that "the instrument of choice is almost always the human instrument." QDR would thus produce contextually rich "vicarious experiences" from "shared constructions" produced by the relationship between researcher and subject (Guba 1993, p. xi).

Using a naturalistic paradigm, a researcher would expect to:

- *Attend to social context* (e.g., time, place, circumstances, culture, development status, type of disaster, population dynamics, community character, etc.) as a critical act that enriches the study (Erlandson et al. 1993, p. 5).
  One example comes from qualitative studies of relocation. Perry and Lindell (1997) studied Allenville, Arizona,

where citizens chose a government "buyout" or relocation to reduce risks associated with a potential dam collapse. The predominantly African American community of 35 homes moved to a new location out of harm's way. Key to the relocation was a local board that connected residents to responsible government agencies. One of the agencies opened a local office in order to keep homeowners informed about the process. During a temporary relocation, homeowners, board members, and government representatives stayed in contact with each other and maintained open lines of communication. Relocatees reported overall satisfaction with their new location, which occurred in a pre-disaster phase. In contrast, city officials in Princeville, North Carolina, declined a buyout offer in a closely contested decision. The African American community, mostly older, retired women living on Social Security, shared strong ties across the 900-plus homes. Their legacy included living in a town formerly known as "Freedom Hill," the first town in the United States incorporated by freed slaves. Local officials and residents felt strongly about saving their historic legacy, one defended repeatedly for decades against violent attacks, economic difficulties, and racial segregation. In these two scenarios, the social, political, historic, and economic context explained the difference in reactions to relocation options. Exceptionally strong place attachment ties in Princeville kept people in place. Government agencies and supportive organizations responded to this sense of place by raising funds, elevating homes, cleaning storm drainage pathways, and strengthening the levee to save the historic location (Phillips, Stukes, Jenkins 2012).

- For naturalistic researchers, *multiple realities exist* (Lincoln and Guba 1985; Erlandson et al. 1993). The lived experience of an event needs to be uncovered and from perspectives crossing an array of social actors. Why were so many people on the roofs of their homes after Hurricane Katrina slammed into the U.S. Gulf Coast in 2005? Disaster researchers who studied the event found that it was not because of popular notions that people were irresponsible or ignored official mandates to leave. One qualitative study concluded that leaving depended "on their contexts and available resources" (Tuason, Güss, and Carroll 2012). Interviews confirmed that people did not understand the path of the storm or that acute poverty impeded evacuation. Furthermore, a mandatory evacuation order from a local authority figure came just twelve hours before the storm slammed into the region. Many living in the urban area lacked transportation to flee and officials did not fully activate plans for public transportation. Levees failed twenty-four hours after the mandatory evacuation order for New Orleans. The city flooded, including parking lots full of buses that could have been used to move people to safety. People with disabilities, senior citizens, and families without cars climbed into their attics and, if capable, hacked through the ceiling with an axe. Though some survivors made it through to the roof or waded through perilous flood waters, at least 1,300 perished along the U.S. Gulf Coast.

- Naturalistic inquiry also encourages a "research design that emanates from the research itself" (Erlandson et al. 1993, 69). This means that *QDR evolves during the data collection and analysis process.* For qualitative research, analysis begins at the moment of data collection as the researcher examines information coming in and fine-tunes the research project. Spradley (1980) describes this process as the "Developmental Research Sequence," in which the researcher begins by asking "what's going on here" and then hones in to understand the social situation, social process, or interactions underway. Naturalism also allows the researcher to keep improving the sample and the research process itself. The consequence is a more focused study and more cost-effective outcome. Imagine, for example, going to an area stricken by a tsunami. One would naturally assume that local officials conducted search and rescue efforts and they probably did—but once arriving on site, the researcher might discover that others became involved, too, including nearby medical staff, neighbors, bystanders, faith-based organizations, and family. In the 2004 Indian Ocean tsunami, for example, rescue of survivors and retrieval of the deceased involved hundreds of elected officials, private citizens, military units, appointed personnel, and volunteers. Choosing the sample beforehand would have proven far too limiting and resulted in a loss of critical data (Scanlon 2006; Hyrapiet 2006).

The emergent process often nonplusses those ingrained with conventional approaches. Yet for QDR, the emergent process often permits the discovery of critical insights that not only advance theory but offer promising, evidence-based best practices. Erlandson et al. (1993, p. 69) offer an eight-step process that walks researchers through designing a naturalistic study. Applied to QDR, an emergent, naturalistic paradigm can yield sound findings (see Table 2.1).

Ethical Issues

The first question that should always be asked for any type of study is: Should the study be done at all? Research should be conducted for the primary purpose of moving forward the body of knowledge on a given topic. Research should not be conducted to secure publications, obtain a degree, or pursue tenure—unless the research contributes to efforts that, for example, expand knowledge, improve practice, or analyze policies. In short, intellectual merit and social benefits should outweigh any personal benefits of the proposed research. Feminist methodologists suggest that such non-reciprocal relationships exploit subjects. Researchers then benefit from such knowledge-extraction while subjects become objectified. At the heart of the debate lies the power that researchers exercise over participants, their contributions, and how the participants come to be viewed. Ethical standards safeguard the rights and experiences of those who choose to participate. However, researchers should "take extra precautions not to betray the trust so freely given" (Fonow and Cook 1991, p. 8). In this section, we first review general parameters for ethical research followed by a discussion of disaster research ethics.

Table 2.1
The Emergent Process of the Naturalistic Paradigm for QDR

STEP	Explanation and Example
1. Entry.	Researchers must first negotiate entry to a site. For quick response research, researchers should have a good reason to be there and impact those affected. Establishing a relationship with those likely to be affected pre-impact can make a significant difference with entry or researchers may need to conduct a two-stage entry process. Those affected may be overwhelmed with workloads or caring for affected family members—or they may be completely open to inquiries. Being flexible means the difference between concluding or continuing the study. Securing entry during non-emergency response times may be far easier to gain entry though the topic may limit access (e.g., homeland security topics, terrorism studies).
2. Sampling.	Experts recommend a purposive sample where you choose carefully who to interview. You would not want to miss a key interviewee who did not get chosen in a random sample (e.g., the emergency manager or fire chief). Snowball sampling then leads researchers to promising others who can fill in the rest of the evacuation story, about life in the shelter, or the reconstruction process. Not only people should be sampled, but sites as well. A wildfire site that started from lightning, for example, might differently affect survivors than one initiated by arson. Those living in the wildfire zone, on the fringe, or simply in the smoky exterior will also experience multiple realities.

Table 2.1
(Continued)

STEP	Explanation and Example
3. Plan for data collection.	Here, the time frame is key for QDR. It is possible to design a quick response research project in advance and then wait (sometimes years) for the right event to unfold and allow the research question to be examined. One can also put together an experienced disaster research team, enter the field with a relevant research question. and conduct a meaningful study (for a listing visit www.colorado.edu/hazards and the Quick Response Report Series). Flexibility must characterize studies, though—even for longer-term projects. In California after the 1989 Loma Prieta earthquake, instability in the mountains (coupled with a drought) meant that researchers (and homeowners) had to wait for years (and rain) to determine if rebuilding could begin.
4. Plan for data analysis.	Numerous authors concur that data analysis begins at the start of any qualitative project (e.g., see Lofland et al. 2006). Most disaster research field study teams conduct daily debriefings to review the data that have been collected, the initial findings, and to determine the next few days' of data collection efforts. Initial analysis can be relatively straightforward, such as domain analysis, which then unfolds systematically to generate deeper and more nuanced insights (Spradley 1980; see later in this book). Scanlon's study (see Chapter 1) of Prince's work on the 1917 Halifax explosion took years and led him through archives, to family members, and into libraries as he slowly identified and filled in holes of the first disaster scholar's work.

(continued)

Table 2.1
(Continued)

STEP	Explanation and Example
5. Plan for quality.	Trustworthiness and credibility mean that researchers need to incorporate steps that result in reputable results (see steps listed later in this chapter). Debriefing with the team members helps with this—as does returning initial findings to interviewees as a "member check." Desmond's (2007) study of wildland firefighters did so, with interviewees commenting on the written draft of what became a published book, *On the Fireline*.
6. Disseminate Findings.	Good researchers disseminate their findings to build the body of knowledge and to yield societal benefits. Many QDRs live a double life by writing not only scholarly works for academic journals but also creating user-friendly materials for practitioners and agencies. Stough and Sharp (2008) generated qualitative insights on case management for people with disabilities after Katrina. They first produced a report for the National Disability Rights Network and subsequently published in a scholarly journal (Stough et al. 2010).
7. Logistical planning.	QDR necessarily involves scheduling interviews, observations, and site visits (including archives and visual documentation) which may require some effort. The quick response time, while access may be gained, may also result in frustration as key people cannot be found, were replaced by new people or organizations, or experienced displacement. Funding must also be secured. Team travel plans need to be scheduled (and rescheduled). Personnel may come and go on a project (as students graduate). Tables 2.2 and 2.3 provide overviews of logistical plan elements.

Table 2.1 (Continued)	
STEP	**Explanation and Example**
8. Review the design.	For QDR, new conditions arise all the time to challenge researchers. Hurricane season in the United States (or cyclone season elsewhere) means that storms may continually disrupt access to research sites and people. In 2005, Hurricane Rita followed Hurricane Katrina by a mere three weeks. Researchers not only had to get their teams out of harm's way—but back in to the sites. They also had to contend with a new condition—the second storm and its impact on personnel, people, places, and processes under study. However, being flexible meant being able to capture interesting and comparable data. The evacuation difficulties with Katrina resulted in a much larger people-generated evacuation for Rita, particularly in the state of Texas. Motivations to evacuate, complexities in managing transportation arteries, movement of medically fragile populations, pet sheltering, and innovative solutions could all have been studied comparatively with sufficient foresight, team members, and funding. Investigators studying the 2011 Japanese earthquake and tsunami also contended with a threatening nuclear accident. Handling such unanticipated conditions requires constant vigilance and a readiness to alter one's research design.

An Overview of Ethical Concerns

In any kind of research, consideration of the human beings under study should be paramount. Researchers should take great care to insure privacy, confidentiality, and comfort during the research process. Such care has not always been the case, which led to the

rise of Institutional Review Boards (IRBs) at academic institu-
tions and agencies that conduct research. The explosive case that
launched IRBs came to light in the 1960s when the media and the
U.S. Congress learned about a U.S. Public Health Service (USPHS)
study on the untreated effects of syphilis among poor, often illiter-
ate, African American men (Jones 1981).

The study began in 1932 when U.S. Public Health Service
(USPHS) staff began to gather data on the effects of untreated
syphilis on 400 African American sharecroppers and day labor-
ers. What made the study particularly unethical was that a cure
for syphilis became available *during the study* but the USPHS
did not offer treatment—or even tell subjects what disease they
had contracted. Rather, thinking they had something called "bad
blood," the subjects suffered horribly from the experiment and
the disease, including enduring spinal taps without anesthesia.
Symptoms included rashes, chest pains, lesions, and infections,
tumors, ulcers, progressive paralysis, and insanity (Jones 1981).

Dozens of the men died from the disease, which also affected
their wives and children. Learning of the study, the U.S. Congress
conducted public hearings and demanded accountability. As a
consequence, federal agencies adopted the Common Rule in 1991,
which arose out of the 1978 "Belmont Report." Essential elements
include respect, beneficence, and justice (see http://www.hhs.
gov/ohrp/humansubjects/index.html).

The Tuskegee study, as it has come to be known, was only one
of multiple research projects critiqued for misleading subjects.
In 1961, Milgram and associates (1974) created a laboratory setting in which "teachers" (subjects who were duped) instructed
"learners" (confederates of the researcher). When learners failed
to correctly learn a word pairing, the researcher instructed the
teacher to punish the learner with an increasingly strong elec-
tric shock. Although the jolt did not really occur, the teachers
thought they *were* shocking learners and experienced considerable stress. Though the purpose was to determine the lengths to
which an individual might obey authority (such as occurred in
Nazi Germany and other authoritarian regimes), the question
of deceiving subjects arose again. The last study, called Project
Camelot (circa 1964), involved researchers in understanding how
conditions fomenting revolution might occur in South America.
The funder, the U.S. Army, had an obvious interest in identifying

the means by which regime change might or might not occur. Researchers faced critique from their colleagues for participating in such politically motivated studies and the study was cancelled before it even began (Babbie 2010).

Each of these classic studies presents important ethical lessons for disaster researchers. The most important one concerns misleading subjects. Today, most IRBs do not approve deceptive research. In some cases, the actual intent of the study or the content of an instrument or procedure might be obscured to objects should knowledge of the subject potentially bias respondents. In such instances, IRB's must review and approve the use of deception, and the intellectual merits must outweigh any risks to subjects. An example might occur when an IRB approves studying how public safety dispatchers handle unanticipated events in a laboratory setting. The test events (such as an explosion) would not be revealed in order to avoid biasing dispatcher response (Drabek 2002).

To guide thinking about ethical decision-making, several perspectives should be considered. The *absolutist* stance says that disguised research is simply unethical and should not be undertaken at all (Denzin and Lincoln, 1998, pp. 35–40). In contrast, a *deception* model accepts the necessity of misleading others in order to gain insights. A *relativist* stance directs researchers to study topics that emanate from personal biography rather than a strict body of knowledge. Ethical standards, in the relativist approach, flow from individual conscience. Most research and IRB decision-making seems governed by the *contextualist-consequentialist* approach, which is based on several main principles (Denzin and Lincoln 1998). In this approach, the researcher builds a relationship of mutual respect and trust that does not involve deception. Researchers do not coerce subjects in any way and treat participants in an open, honest, and sincere manner (Goode 1996). Researchers must clearly spell out their rights to human subjects, including the right to refuse to participate, to decline to answer any question, or to end their participation at any time.

Beyond these models, feminists call on researchers to foster a non-oppressive relationship between researchers and subjects. To do so, feminists call for "an ethic that stresses personal accountability, caring, the value of individual expressiveness, the capacity for empathy, and the sharing of emotionality" (Eichler 1980; Epstein and Stewart 1991; Fonow and Cook 1991; Reinharz 1992; Denzin and Lincoln 1998; Hesse-Biber and Leavy 2011).

Disaster Research Ethics

Ethics writings over disaster research have surfaced only fairly recently and primarily in the aftermath of terrorist events. In January, 2003, those present at a conference on "Ethical Issues Pertaining to Research in the Aftermath of Disaster" discussed issues of concern and recommended ethical protocol (Collogan et al., 2004). Attendees' first focused on whether disaster research could further harm disaster survivors. Would a disaster, followed by researchers seeking interviews, increase personal trauma?

To manage such concerns, IRB boards typically weigh the risks versus the benefits of proposed research with prospective subjects. In addition to the risks mentioned here, IRBs usually consider whether research will inconvenience subjects, the possibility of legal action, and breach of confidentiality (Collogan et al. 2004; Newman and Kaloupek 2004). Recognizing that "the magnitude of risk to subjects of research post-disaster are largely undocumented," conference participants concluded that non-disaster studies of patients dealing with acute stress "offer evidence that decisional ability in these individuals, as a group, is not significantly compromised" (Collogan, et al. 2004, pp. 364–365). Based on related studies, the conference concluded that people affected by disasters could make rational decisions regarding their participation. Further, conference attendees suggested that assuming disaster survivors might be impaired could be potentially stigmatizing (Rosenstein 2004). Disaster researchers have found similar results, as the majority of those who face disaster respond fairly well psychologically (Norris et al. 2002a and 2002b).

Another concern raised by conference attendees centered on survivors, organizations, and communities that might be overwhelmed by researchers inundating the area. The possibility that researchers might interview a single subject multiple times, for example, arises as a possible (though certainly unintentional) point of exploitation. Imagine, for example, the beleaguered emergency manager with a stack of researchers' business cards on her desk. Demands for her time have been extensive, and an unknown face has now appeared—in the name of science—to conduct a formal interview. Even the most dedicated scholar practitioner might think twice after weeks of sleeplessness. Researchers must understand the response time demands on those affected and plan their studies accordingly. As one experienced researcher recommends, researchers should use the response time to make contact, to gather perishable data as much as possible, and then return for more detailed inquiry (Stallings 2002).

IRBs must also assess the potential benefits of disaster to research participants. Those benefits are presumed to include medical (see Landrigan et al. 2004) and mental health services (see Pfefferbaum, Call and Sconzo 1999), gaining insights, helping survivors feeling more empowered, and serving a broader good through advancing science. The latter may be particularly relevant in a context in which research participation seems to be one's patriotic duty, such as with terrorist events (Collogan et al. 2004). Benefits to participants have not been empirically substantiated but are presumed to exist in both disaster and non-disaster research. In general, an IRB will weigh such benefits versus the risks. After examining comparable studies of how human subjects conducted their own cost-benefit assessment in clinical studies, "it appears the majority of participants in these trauma-related studies report favorable perceptions of the cost-benefit balance" (Newman and Kaloupek 2004, p. 392). Overall, "research participation may upset subjects but it does not traumatize them as a disastrous event would" (Collogan et al. p. 367). To protect subjects in disaster research, standard IRB protocol should apply.

IRBs will require, as based on the Belmont Report, that subjects must be respected. This requires that subjects be informed of the risks, benefits, and procedures they may experience and consent to the research process. Privacy and confidentiality procedures, with appropriate ways to protect human subject data, must be explained to the subject prior to requesting their consent. The research procedures must be clearly spelled out so that subjects can determine if they want to participate. All human subjects must have the right to refuse participation, to decline any question or procedure during the research, and to end their participation without penalty.

Ethical Issues and Terrorism

Terrorist events differ from more common disasters like floods or tornadoes. Terrorism is an act of violence designed to promote fear, undermine economic and political stability, and take lives. Although it is possible to anticipate most floods, tornadoes, or hurricanes, terrorism strikes without warning. Acts of terrorism cause mass exposure to brutal conditions and sights—which have the potential to increase traumatic reactions (North, Pfefferbaum, Tucker 2002). Two terrorist events have focused discussion around the ethics of terrorism-context research: the Oklahoma City bombing of 1995 and the attacks of September 11th, 2001. Both were handled differently.

In Oklahoma City, Oklahoma, an act of terrorism occurred when a domestic terrorist detonated a massive bomb outside the Alfred P. Murrah Federal Building on April 19, 1995. Housing multiple federal and state agencies and a day care center, the bomb tore away an entire side of the structure, claimed the lives of 165 individuals, and produced horrific injuries among survivors. People in adjacent buildings suffered injuries as well, with the concussion of the explosion being felt for miles. Emergency responders spent long hours inside arduous and dangerous conditions searching for trapped survivors and making difficult life-and-death decisions. Massive media coverage amplified the exposure to school children, which increased again as related criminal trials commenced (Pfefferbaum, Call and Sconzo 1999).

Concerned over the arrival of many potential researchers, the Governor of Oklahoma issued a decree that the University of Oklahoma Health Services Center would monitor and approve all studies. The intent of the decree and the review process insured that survivors would not feel pressured to participate in a research effort that could be potentially re-traumatizing (North, Pfefferbaum, Tucker 2002). The IRB also insured efficient data collection to maximize the research benefits. Some of their procedures paired investigators with Oklahoma researchers and clinicians familiar with the local context. Further, the IRB approved "only methodologically acceptable research that either promised direct practical benefits or demonstrated a clearly clinical focus." Researchers could then draw samples from a comprehensive registry of survivors. Children, who automatically fall into the category of a vulnerable population, prompted the IRB to install strict informed consent requirements. Many schools, however—with a potential sample of 16,000 students—did not cooperate. Researchers initially found the process frustrating, yet eventually "bonded into a cooperative research group" (North, Pfefferbaum, Tucker 2002, p. 581).

In contrast, research on the attacks of September 11th "were anything but coordinated" (North, Pfefferbaum, Tucker 2002, p. 582). Conditions varied for researchers and IRBs in this attack, particularly the magnitude of the attacks and multiple sites in New York, Washington D.C., and Pennsylvania. Beyond the attack sites, locations where air traffic controllers grounded airplanes (in the United States and outside) further increased potential research sites. With one of the sites being a military location (The Pentagon), access to conduct research would necessarily be limited. In the aftermath of such a massive event, a centralized IRB failed to appear and most researchers relied on their own internal review boards which generated an extensive number of studies (for an example, see Monday 2003).

As a consequence of experiences with these terrorist events, some additional ethical steps have been identified:

- Develop a two-step process to invite participation. Provide an initial overview during the first contact and a more formal discussion during a second contact (Rosenstein 2004). This type of research may not be as feasible in a rapid response context but may be relevant in traumatic events like terrorism.
- Partner with local researchers to understand local climate and context (North, Pfefferbaum, Tucker 2002; Rosenstein 2004). Local involvement can also open doors when outside researchers arrive in a beleaguered community. For potentially traumatic events, a local partner can identify therapeutic referrals as appropriate. Locals can also explain culture and language so that researchers understand data from the perspective of the subject rather than the assumptions

of the researcher (for an example, see Chapter 1 on tsunami research).

- Train research teams in the process of conducting ethical research, how to identify individuals experiencing stress levels, and how to respond appropriately. Training research teams to deal with their own level of exposure to trauma is also a wise move (Fleischman and Wood 2002).
- Collect data on the impact of the research so that future investigators and IRBs will be able to craft thoughtful and evidence-informed human subject protocols (North et al. 2002; Rosenstein 2004; Collogan et al. 2004).

Additional Ethical Responsibilities

Beyond responsibilities to the human subject, researchers also have additional ethical responsibilities. One responsibility is to the funder of the research to insure rigorous methodological standards and financial accountability. Researchers must accurately and honestly present their findings, and without bending to pressure from their funders. Another dimension of a researcher's responsibility is to the scientific community. We must treat human subjects with respect so that other researchers who arrive after us will find subjects unharmed and willing to participate. My own first interview went very badly and I wondered if I had any academic future. After an hour of trying my best to learn from the participant, he blurted out, "I'm not crazy, you know!" He then explained that a previous researcher had administered tests to him to determine his psychological stability after a massive fatality event. Though it was not clear if the researcher or the test itself had troubled the participant, he certainly felt stigmatized by the research process. It is our job as researchers, as fellow human beings, to insure that such an experience does not occur.

Quick-Response and Longitudinal Research Designs

Disaster researchers conduct "quick response"-type research frequently. In this section, we learn more about how quick-response research occurs and the challenges that investigators face during such times. Longitudinal research occurs far less frequently and is described here to encourage readers to consider engaging in such an under-used but vitally important research choice.

Quick Response Research

Many qualitative disaster studies take place during the response period. Why? Interestingly, disasters reveal the essential nature of human societies (Taylor 1977). When we are experiencing our worst day, for example, others often respond as fellow human beings committed to relieving suffering. Altruistic behavior permeates the response period, seen so easily in what has been termed personnel and material convergence (Fritz and Mathewson 1957b and c), or the arrival of spontaneous, unaffiliated volunteers (also called SUVs) and unsolicited donations. Disaster also "lays bare" the social problems of our society, enabling researchers to understand how social inequities expose people to disproportionate losses (Barton 1970). The response period represents a critical stage in the life-cycle of disasters, often followed by extraordinary efforts to recover, heightened interest in mitigation, and enhanced levels of preparedness. By not capturing response period data, critical information can be lost that will influence analysis of response activities and how well we understand later stages in the life-cycle of emergency management. For example, knowing how much disruption occurred to key infrastructure and lifelines and where it occurred (e.g., power, water, sewage communications) can enable a researcher to understand community recovery patterns.

One can thus conduct "firehouse" (i.e., be ready to go) field research either as a phase-specific study (response) or as the initial step in a longitudinal research design. The key is to be ready when disaster strikes. Such a stance may feel uncomfortable to more deductively oriented researchers, but qualitative investigators working from an inductive approach can take advantage of the seeming suddenness of disasters.

And, rather than coming as a complete surprise, it is actually possible to anticipate general locations where hazards exist and to plan a research project accordingly. For example, being ready to conduct a study on business disruption in an area of high seismic or tornado activity seems reasonable, although the researcher may have to wait until an appropriate event occurs. A researcher can design an interview instrument, secure approval from an IRB,

Table 2.2

A Quick-Response Logistical Plan

Date	Events
Day 1	Firestorm breaks out. Team members monitor conditions, locations, people impacted, and organizations involved as events unfold. Researchers collect social media, communication reports, documents, and begin to develop an initial sampling frame for people, places, organizations. Team leaders notify the team to stand by for deployment, check field data collection kits, pack their bags, and get some sleep.
Day 2	The team determines that the firestorm fits conceptual criteria for a "disaster" and requests activation of their quick response grant. Team heads to the sites affected with IRB forms, data collection instruments and tools to record data, and insignia identifying their team and purpose. Reconnaissance begins to determine points of entry (if not pre-established) and where the team can sleep and eat. Places visited link to the research design. For an evacuation study, team members seek out first responders and emergency managers involved in issuing warnings and routing traffic, then move to public shelters. Finding those affected utterly exhausted, the team explains their purpose and identifies a time frame to return (or, where possible, launches interviews, observations, and continues to collect documents, visual data).
Days 2–3	Team debriefs nightly and, when possible, during the day to determine the quality and quantity of data, the logical "next steps," and the initial findings. The team fine tunes their sample, determines feasibility of next steps, and spends lengthy time processing their data where and when possible (trying always to never let a night go before recording and processing data).

(continued)

RESEARCH DESIGN : 45

Table 2.2 (Continued)	
Date	**Events**
Days 3–4	Ideally, interviews and observations continue along with document collection and visual collection. Logs develop of the kind of data, contacts made, and people available for a return visit. Nightly debriefings continue. Likely sites include EOC, shelters, respite areas, ICS sites for hot spots, faith-based organizations, etc.
Days 5–6	Continue data collection and analysis, lay foundation for a return visit to the area. Data are always carried out of the affected area with backups and are secured per IRB criteria.
Days 7–14	Team regroups to transcribe and analyze data, plan out the next trip, catch up on sleep, orient the next team, and where/when possible, secure time slots for interviews and observations.
Day 15	Second team deploys (as funding allows), hopefully to a more predictable environment for data collection and analysis.

and secure research funds prior to an event. Then, when a disaster fitting within appropriate parameters occurs, the field team can deploy expeditiously (see Table 2.2).

Failure to enter the field quickly may imperil the project. In the dynamic environment of an unfolding disaster, perceptions of events may change or be forgotten. Capturing those perceptions must occur soon after onset, preferably in the context in which they occur, and as they unfold. After Hurricane Andrew occurred in 1992, one of our teams watched as the American Red Cross set up operations in a large auditorium. The first day, our team saw the arrival of key, experienced disaster organizations. As the days unfolded, we mapped when new organizations arrived and where they set up their tables. Mapping allowed us to see when local organizations intermeshed with external organizations in order to provide service delivery to an exceptionally diverse area (Phillips, Garza, Neal 1994). We saw a similar pattern unfold after

Hurricane Katrina at the FEMA Joint Field Office (JFO) in Baton Rouge. Originally organized into one floor of a department store, the JFO ultimately expanded into multiple floors and an adjacent building. Clearly, FEMA needed space to set up working areas for the National Response Framework's Emergency Support Functions (NRF, ESFs) as additional personnel arrived.

As another reason to conduct quick response research, practitioners may not save relevant data. In such cases data can "perish" (Michaels 2003). Imagine, for example, an Emergency Operations Center (EOC). Within most EOCs, desks are arranged to accommodate different ESFs (e.g., EFS#6 Mass Care, ESF#8 Public Health, or ESF#14 Long Term Recovery, see http://www.fema. gov/national-response-framework). Each ESF usually has an assigned area with a desk(s) where people take notes (on paper or in an electronic log) as events unfold. Imagine the value of such documents: They could reveal the chronology of an event, the ways in which ESFs communicate, and the types of tasks that develop. It would be possible, for example, to determine a timeline of when certain tasks should occur, which could ultimately inform research on planning and improve Emergency Operations Plans (EOPs).

Securing funding for rapid response research can be challenging. Many researchers rely on internal funds from their universities and colleges or on personal funds to reach the field. Two other sources have been used historically in the field. The first comes from the U.S. National Science Foundation Rapid Response Research (RAPID) grant program (similar to a previous program called Small Grants for Exploratory Research or SGER). In past decades, researchers have used such funds to gather perishable data and then submit proposals for additional funding. Major events may trigger a special call for needed research. In 2012, for example, debris from the Japanese tsunami began to wash ashore along the western coast of North America. The National Science Foundation issued a notice that funds had become available for related research (see Box 2.1).

A second commonly-used source is the Quick Response Grant program at the Natural Hazards Research and Applications Information Center (NHRAIC, often called The Natural Hazards Center) in the University of Colorado at Boulder. Their goal is to provide:

Funds for researchers to quickly travel to disaster-affected areas to capture perishable data. In addition to expanding

Box 2.1   **National Science Foundation RAPID Research**

. . . .

"In the aftermath of the March 2011 earthquake and subsequent tsunami in Japan, fields of debris are now washing up on the western shores of the United States. According to the National Oceanic and Atmospheric Administration (NOAA), Japanese authorities say that approximately five million tons of wreckage flowed into the Pacific Ocean following the earthquake and tsunami. While a majority of it likely sank, experts estimate that between one to two million tons was left floating and is heading toward North America. The debris fields are expected to reach and potentially threaten the west coast of North America from the spring of 2012 through late 2014. When unforeseen circumstances offer unique opportunities to advance basic knowledge, NSF has in place the Rapid Response Research (RAPID) funding mechanism. As noted in the Grant Proposal Guide (GPG), this mechanism is used to support activities having a severe urgency with regard to availability of, or access to, data, facilities or specialized equipment, including quick-response research on natural or anthropogenic disasters and similar unanticipated events. In the past, RAPID funding supported fundamental research activities related to acute events such as the New Zealand earthquake in February 2011, the earthquake and tsunami in Japan in March 2011, and the Deepwater Horizon oil spill in 2010.

The NSF Directorates for Biological Sciences (BIO), Geosciences (GEO), Engineering (ENG), Mathematical and Physical Sciences (MPS), and Computer & Information Science & Engineering (CISE), and the Office of Cyberinfrastructure (OCI) are accepting proposals to conduct research on the potential threat to the North American west coast from debris fields associated with the March 2011 Japanese earthquake and tsunami. Proposals must conform to the guidelines for preparation of Rapid Response Research (RAPID) proposals as specified in the NSF Grant Proposal Guide (GPG) available at: http://www.nsf.gov/publications/pub_summ. jsp?ods_key=gpg." Source: Verbatim from the National Science Foundation, http://www.nsf.gov/pubs/2012/nsf12116/nsf12116.jsp, last accessed February 2013).

academic knowledge, funded researchers submit brief reports that make preliminary analyses of recent events available to the Hazards Center's multidisciplinary network of researchers, practitioners, and educators. The program promotes innovation in disaster research by favoring students, new researchers, and novel areas of study (for more, visit http://www.colorado.edu/hazards/research/qr/).

Proposals to NHRAIC are fairly short, usually under three pages, and often target specific areas of concern to the nation such as social vulnerability, mass fatalities, historic preservation, evacuations, food security, and debris removal. Most grants provide about $2,000 of funding. Nearly 100 final project reports can be found at the Natural Hazard Center's Quick Response Research website (website as noted above).

Regardless of the source of funding, several key principles should guide any rapid response research:

- Advance contacts should be made prior to a disaster. Doing so increases the likelihood that researchers will be able to enter affected areas, find the people they need to interview, and secure needed data.
- IRB approval should be obtained prior to any formal data-gathering used for reports, theses, dissertations, or publications. Some IRBs also require approval for reconnaissance trips to insure that potential subjects receive consistent messages about the study and their possible participation. IRB protocol should be sufficiently robust to take into account varying field circumstances. For example, one may enter the field wanting to conduct interviews but discover that only observation is possible. The IRB should have pre-approved both. Or, you may discover additional types of personnel that need to be interviewed. An IRB-approved sampling frame should anticipate such additions.
- Field kits for data-gathering should be developed in advance of any team deployment. Field kits should include business cards and identification tags for personnel and vehicles; brochures on one's academic home; lists of possible contacts and research sites; IRB

forms; data collection instruments (e.g., interview guides, observation checklists); paper and utensils for notes; electronic tools (cameras, computers, pads, digital pens) for recording information and developing field reports; cell phones and a back-up system should cell communications be out; extra batteries, car chargers, and back-up systems for data-gathering should the power be out; extra clothing, and where needed, food, water, and bedding (based in part on Quarantelli 2002).

- Rigorous research methodology should apply despite the seeming informality or dynamic quality of many response settings. Researchers should maintain their stance as an investigator.

- Researchers should understand that possible participants may be exhausted and may not be able to provide time or usable insights. In such circumstances, it is wise to make a contact and then return for data-collection at a later point (Stallings 2006). Researcher convergence may also become a problem, particularly in major events (Michaels 2003). Investigators shoulder ethical responsibility to the scientific community to not unduly impact possible participants. You may need to work collaboratively with disaster colleagues to reduce the overall impact on participants (North, Pfefferbaum, Tucker 2002).

- Travel into the area may be hazardous and teams should prepare for physical and mental challenges. It may be difficult to secure lodging, so research teams should attempt to do so before arrival or expect to drive significant distances into affected areas. Lodging should never be secured at the expense of locally affected populations.

- Nightly debriefings should occur within the field team and with members outside of the affected area (e.g., a thesis or dissertation advisor). Updates to instruments, sampling procedures (people and places), and research methods should be considered.

- Team members should conserve time to write up field notes and interview summaries while in the field and memories remain fresh.

- Team members should eat well, hydrate, and rest.

- Once back from the field, an overview field trip report should be generated. Quarantelli (2002) indicates the report should be 3–10 pages in length and include information on the event and the field team members. The report should describe the physical and social impacts of the disaster, the general geographic area and related physical features, demographics of the people, descriptions of the organizations and units involved, and general answers to the main research questions. The interview guide can be used as a means to organize impressions of the data, including any initial data analysis undertaken while in the field. The report should capture the quality and quantity of the data, identify additional people and places that require further study, and offer recommendations on next steps to be taken. A list of the people interviewed, the places observed, the photos taken, and the documents collected should be appended.

Longitudinal Research

Longitudinal research, which occurs over lengthy periods of time, remains rare in disaster research. Primary reasons for the lack of such studies include an historic focus on response time periods noted earlier (which usually ends within days to weeks), lack of funding for multi-year projects, faculty needs to publish or perish, students who must complete degree requirements, and attrition among people and organizations affected by disasters. Finding people and organizations to study may prove challenging, as disasters cause displacement and frequent moves among affected residents. Organizations, like search and rescue teams, enter and leave areas quickly. Because they may be based away from the research team, following such teams from one disaster to the next can be significant in terms of time, staffing, and travel funds.

No standard exists for the specific length of time that constitutes a longitudinal study. The research question should drive such a decision, particularly those that look at change over time (Saldaña 2003). For example, how long does it take before displaced residents can secure permanent housing? Logic suggests considerable differences among people based on income levels, insurance coverage, disaster-related job losses, age, and the availability of recovery organizations and volunteers to help rebuild. People with insurance and sufficient resources may be able to rebuild quickly—depending on damage—while those with less may languish for years. At the five-year mark after Hurricane Katrina, for example, 860 Louisiana residents remained in federally funded trailers, doubled or tripled up with other family, in rental units, or had permanently relocated to an entirely different city or state. The New Orleans population had yet to rebound fully, with 100,000 residents still not home (Greater New Orleans Community Data Center 2010).

Qualitative researchers often pursue an understanding of processes or the steps and stages that unfold across time. Disaster research is no different. Quarantelli (1982), for example, unfurled a four-stage model of sheltering and housing across time. Emergency sheltering (tents, overpasses, cars) occurs first and somewhat rapidly in most cases. Temporary sheltering (Red Cross shelters, relief camps) then becomes established. Most temporary sheltering closes fairly soon, yet studies show variation. People with disabilities lingered in post-Katrina shelters in the United States for months while awaiting accessible, federally-funded housing (NOD 2005; NCD 2009). The 2010 Haiti earthquake displaced 1.5 million who went into 1,300 relief camps around Port-au-Prince. Nearly three years later, 24% (357,700) remained in the camps (USAID 2012). Temporary housing occurs when displaced persons can re-establish a household routine, such as cooking and cleaning. This phase may take days, months, or even years while reconstruction goes on. Permanent housing can also result within days for the lucky—or half a decade or more for those less fortunate. Longitudinal researchers need to be able to capture not only these phases, but the ways in which variations occur across populations.

Bell (2008) uncovered information about the process of displacement experienced by Katrina survivors. Well over 8,000 survivors landed in Austin, Texas, a city that lacked experience or sufficient case managers to help those displaced. Bell (with colleagues) interviewed 78 people, observed at over 50 public meetings, and continued the research from December of 2005 through December 2006. She documented the struggle of survivors as they transitioned from the familiar culture and comfort of New Orleans and Louisiana to the unfamiliar location and new culture of Austin and Texas. Case managers also needed to understand the culture of the survivors who had lost their connections to not only people, but familiar food, accents, manners, and events. Bell's long-term research also demonstrated the psychological impact that losing familiar faces and places had on people's abilities to rebound. Bell uncovered the challenges faced by both survivors and case managers as they tried to find normalcy again, in a system overtaxed with thousands of newly arriving people traumatized by disaster (see also Weber and Peek 2012).

An even longer study came from a ten-year look back at Hurricane Andrew (Dash et al. 2007). Studying the consequences of the 1992 southern Florida storm for working-class families, researchers reached out to the 208 original study participants from 1993. Dash and colleagues made a concerted effort to find the original study participants. To do so, they sent flyers and made at least three visits to survivor's homes, eventually finding 85 of the 208 and securing data from 32. Echoing concerns over attrition for longitudinal studies, 108 had moved out of the area and another 17 remained unavailable. Dash and colleagues (2007, p. 15) reflected:

> Several factors may explain the low response rate, including the length of time since the first interview, and thus lessened interest in the topic, reluctance to talk about what remained a painful topic, concerns about home repairs and reconstruction that may not meet zoning requirements, unavailability due to work commitments, and fear prompted by a series of home invasions reported in the local media. Women were somewhat more likely to refuse to participate. Interviews were conducted in English or Spanish.

The 32 respondents participated in a short survey and an open-ended interview. Over time, the research within this working-class community revealed that about two-thirds lived in damaged homes while going through repairs—and that many described the reconstruction work as less than adequate. Some felt taken advantage of by unscrupulous contractors and undertook repairs themselves. They felt physically and emotionally exhausted and quite a few reported a lingering trauma from surviving the storm.

Mitchell (2008) reflected on a 1976 earthquake in Tangshan, China, a city located about 100 miles east of Beijing. On July 28 of that year, a 7.8 Richter magnitude earthquake destroyed the city of one million people. About 90% of the buildings collapsed. Nearly a quarter million, or one-fourth of the city's residents, perished in the event. Another 164,000 sustained serious injuries. In 2004, Mitchell visited the area, seeing a "model of what can be accomplished by introduction of appropriate architecture, engineering, and physical planning" (Mitchell 2008, p. 26). Though parts of the reconstruction remained incomplete and somewhat critiqued, a centralized government approach had spurred rebuilding. One noteworthy aspect included the presence of 3,917 survivors with disabilities who were living in 18 long term care facilities. The reconstruction, fueled by a strong government approach, also sped forward due to broader social and economic forces. China entered the global economy in the 1980s. Reconstruction within Tangshan and goods coming out of revitalized Tangshan industries helped to speed the recovery. Much of this came on the heels of China "opening up" after U.S. President Nixon's visit there in the 1970s. In short, a longitudinal perspective enabled Mitchell to see the physical labor effort, the national-level infusion of funds and planning, and the broader global trends that influenced rebuilding this major city so successfully.

Longitudinal research occurs over time (see Table 2.3). Studies can be micro-focused at the individual level or macro-level including analysis of conditions that influence reconstruction. Other phases can be examined as well, such as the process of mitigation planning or policy-making, efforts to design, train and exercise emergency operations plans, or public education efforts around a particular hazard. Several key principles can guide such inquiry:

- Longitudinal research must be covered by IRB protocol, which will probably require yearly updates.
- It is wise to anticipate new conditions that will influence research. Hurricanes have a tendency to strike the same areas over time. People studying Katrina, for example, had to contend with Rita (also in 2005), Ike (2008), and Isaac (2012). The Deepwater Horizon Oil spill affected the same area as did a steep economic downturn.
- Rigorous methodology should characterize longitudinal studies. Because researchers may come to know communities and study participants fairly well over time, it is wise to remember one's role as researcher and to continually reflect upon researcher-subject relationships.

Table 2.3
A Pre-Planned but Flexible Longitudinal Logistical Plan

Date	Events
Early August	City announces effort to conduct Mitigation Planning and invites stakeholders to the planning table. Researchers secure access at the planning meetings and a list of the stakeholders (with IRB approval).
September through May	Researchers observe monthly meetings and conduct interviews with stakeholders at relevant intervals. Team also collects documents including minutes from meetings, media reports, and drafts of the mitigation plan. An increasingly narrowed focus emerges from general mitigation planning to the participatory process in identifying priorities for hazard reduction.
May–June	Researchers observe how the planning committee presents the plan to the public and solicits their input. Observations are held at public events, data are collected from social media, and interviews with those who attend the public events begin.
July	Researchers observe as the plan is presented to the City Council for approval followed by interviews with city council members regarding their perceptions of the public participation process.
August	The city submits the plan to the state or federal agency for approval. The researchers then schedule interviews within these agencies. During these interviews, a presidential election is held and key leaders of the agency are replaced with new political appointments. A new philosophy emerges governing public participation which is followed, documented, and analyzed by the research team.
June	The relevant agency rejects the mitigation plan for failing to include people with disabilities and new immigrants to the area who did not speak English.

(continued)

Date	Events
Table 2.3 **(Continued)**	
Post June	The team returns to the original city location to follow reactions and rapidly integrates new team members with an understanding of disability access and participation as well as researchers who speak Spanish and Vietnamese. New interviews are conducted among Spanish-speaking individuals and people with disabilities who are now part of the mitigation planning effort. A new team member joins who can conduct interviews in sign language. Attempts to secure interviews with Vietnamese Americans fail due to fear associated with signing IRB forms. Researchers contact local religious authorities and advocacy groups and attempt to build a working relationship in order to conduct focus groups with Vietnamese-speaking residents.

- Attempts to follow study participants should occur at regular intervals to avoid significant attrition. Researchers should work to maintain the interest and motivation of study participants over time.
- Funding must be carefully conserved to last the full duration of a longitudinal study, planning for possible increases in the costs of travel and staff time.
- Lead investigators must work diligently to meet the needs of research team members. Faculty members will need to publish (to secure raises, tenure, and promotion) and students will need to graduate. Staff attrition over time will require the addition of new team members who will need to be trained on the project.
- Study participants should be given periodic updates or reports on the progress of the study. Researchers should reflect carefully on the potential impact of such reports which may influence study participants.

Sampling

Choosing whom to talk to, where and what to observe, when to go to a setting, and which type of event—as well as which visual image to record and what document to select is determined by the process of sampling. Researchers rely on two different strategies to select subjects, sites, and materials: probability and non-probability sampling. Though most qualitative disaster research relies on non-probability sampling, both will be discussed in this section.

Probability Sampling

Probability sampling relies on standardized techniques to ensure that researchers choose participants, locations, or documents without bias. The process begins by generating a sampling frame, which is a list of all potential interviewees, sites, images or documents (hereafter simply referred to as participants unless otherwise noted). Securing the sampling frame, particularly under disaster conditions, may be challenging. It may be difficult to impossible to obtain an accurate list of all residents in a given shelter. Privacy and confidentiality laws may prohibit such disclosure. Further, evacuees usually move into and out of the shelter fairly rapidly. Such turnover means that capturing a representative sample at any point in time may not be feasible. Or, consider a wildfire in progress. Geo-locating which fire department is on which fire in a rapidly-moving, rapid-onset event may be impossible even with dispatcher logs.

Consistent within probability sampling is the use of a random selection process. To illustrate, think about a list of residents in a community damaged by a tornado. This sampling frame, which could potentially contain tens of thousands of people to interview, needs to be honed down. Reasons for limiting the sample include cost and time needed to do the interviews. To insure that everyone has an equal probability of selection, researchers use a *random sampling strategy*. The process begins by numbering those listed in the sampling frame, then using a table of random numbers to identify which numbers to pick. Using this process, a fairly representative sample can be taken from the larger population with less bias. Each sample has the potential to vary somewhat from the larger population (and from each sample drawn) which can be countered by increasing the size of the sample.

One study of shelters used another probability sampling method after Hurricane Katrina (Phillips, Wikle, Head, Pike 2012). To do so, researchers generated a list of shelters collected from various public sources. After culling shelters that turned out to be for first responders, shelter staff, or pets, the list resulted in a total of 626 potentially open shelters. To insure that all types of shelters were captured in the final sample, the researchers relied on *stratified random sampling* to sort the shelters into relevant "strata": (1) Red Cross and non-Red Cross sites and (2) location by state (46 in Texas, 361 in Louisiana, and 189 in Mississippi). The shelters were then enumerated within the strata and sites were chosen using a table of random numbers. In this way, the study used probability theory to select a smaller sample from the larger population. The final sample included 9 shelters in Texas, 49 in Louisiana, and 24 in Mississippi. (n = 82). Some degree of confidence can then be taken that the shelter sample could be generalized to the fuller list of shelters. Because time, funding and rapidly closing shelters meant that all shelters could not be visited, the sampling procedure was a good choice.

In another example, researchers wanted to understand perceptions of aid in various nation-states after the 2004 Indian Ocean tsunami (Letukas and Barnshaw 2008). They started by determining appropriate newspapers in the United States (the largest western donor), along with India, Thailand, and Indonesia (heavily affected nations). The sample was further delimited to English-language newspapers with significant amounts of coverage. The study covered the time period from the day of the tsunami (December 26, 2004) for 365 days. Using three search terms, they identified 6,168 news articles. After eliminating articles for duplication, relevance, and content, 2,084 articles remained. To reduce the sample further, they used *systematic sampling* or every n^{th} case. Researchers reduced the total number by choosing every second article resulting in 1,054 articles (355 from the United States, 273 Indian, 238 Indonesian, and 188 Thai).

Probability sampling techniques result in choosing cases (places, people, events) without bias. However, doing so can also compromise qualitative disaster research as the process could miss those most needed in the sample: emergency managers, elected officials, key community leaders, certain survivors, those involved in relevant tasks (animal rescue, shelter management, long-term recovery). Accordingly, non-probability sampling accommodates such problems.

Non-Probability Sampling

Non-probability methods to choose samples are more likely to be used in qualitative disaster research than probability methods. Naturalistic paradigms in particular call for an emergent sampling design which cannot be drawn in advance (Lincoln and Guba 1985). Rather, the fieldwork process reveals the next participant, site, or document that needs to be sampled. This strategy, called an emergent sampling design, is based on serial selection in which the researcher selects the next case based on the first case. This process allows the researcher to continually focus the sample and efficiently leads the researcher to the point of *theoretical saturation* (Lincoln and Guba 1985; Richardson 1987). This point, at which a researcher can predict fairly accurately what the next respondent will say, represents the point of closure for the study or the point at which it is necessary to diversify the sample to increase breadth of understanding.

Most disaster researchers rely on standardized techniques used in qualitative research more generally. Probably the most-used technique is *snowball sampling*, where the researcher asks the person they interviewed to recommend another person who can also shed light on the research question. Snowball sampling is particularly well-suited to study the interconnectedness of networks and to produce depth on a given topic. Conversely, snowball sampling can result in gleaning a one-sided view of a topic. Care must therefore be taken to ensure that sufficient diversity of thought has been captured, rather than falling into a homogeneous pool of like-minded participants.

Other non-probability sampling techniques include purposive or judgmental sampling along with quota sampling. Purposive or judgmental sampling focuses the researcher on the people, places, or events that fit a pre-defined criteria. For example, asking someone to refer you to the EOC personnel who manage Facebook or twitter feeds increases the chance you will interview the person most relevant to your social media study (Stallings 2002). Quota sampling relies on pre-determined

categories of persons. Someone wanting to study first responders, for example, might be advised to include people who fit into
the categories of law enforcement, firefighting, police, emergency medical, and dispatching.

Beyond the number of people to sample, researchers also need
to consider the type of person they should contact. Snowball
sampling directs you to prospective interviewees who can shed
insight—but it is also worthwhile to diversify the sample by the
type of person. For example, someone new to the EOC, fire house,
or recovery team might see events quite differently than a veteran.
Their fresh perspective can reveal additional dimensions of a setting that someone with 20 years in the location might not see as
readily. Similarly, researchers should consider native as well as
very informed persons. What those in a core group know likely
differs from what those on the periphery know, a condition that
can influence group commitment, participation, trust, and credibility (Quarantelli 1985).

Sampling techniques do not vary for disaster studies. However,
disaster studies do require consideration of additional key elements of a disaster study including site selection, time, and events.

Site Selection

Hazards cause disasters in often-predictable locations. Researchers
can identify earthquake fault lines as possible sites for research,
as well as areas at risk for repetitive flooding, volcanic action, or
tornadoes. Hazards alone, and the physical damage they cause,
do not necessarily equal a "disaster" as discussed in Chapter 1.
Given significant social disruption, a disaster—or even a catastrophe—can become an event to study. What researchers seek out,
though, is not necessarily the hazard itself and probably not even
the physical damage. Rather, social scientists who conduct fire and
disaster research seek sites where social activities, social processes,
and social actors interact with the physical and built environment. Research questions drive the selection of appropriate sites
to conduct interviews or observations, or to gather documents or
visual data. An area heavily damaged by an earthquake is therefore
not necessarily the location of research. Rather, a scientist might
examine policy-making in a distant state or provincial capital
related to mitigation of future earthquake risks.

A number of considerations drive site selection. If the impact zone is the desired location, and quick response research is desired, then researchers may have to seek sites where entry can be achieved (Marshall and Rossman 1998). Moving into an affected area may require pre-negotiated credentials to move past barricades and into secured areas. Navigating past such gate-kept locations has become increasingly difficult in recent years, especially given security concerns that developed after September 11th. Even in a situation where terrorism is not the event under study, military troops and police have prevented researchers from entry. Your gatekeeper could be the Public Information Officer (PIO) at the EOC, the National Guard troop limiting access to the shelter, or the head of the neighborhood association who does not want any more people bothering residents struggling to rebuild. Different contexts also matter. Conducting research after the 2004 Indian Ocean tsunami meant securing access in a variety of political settings. Both researchers and humanitarians had to contend with a separatist military organization called the Tamil Tigers in Sri Lanka. Sites that involve acts of terrorism or crime (mass fatalities, wildfire-related arson) are likely to limit researcher access significantly.

Gaining access to a site thus influences site selection. Securing credentials or letters of authorization from a funder may not be enough—and may require extensive advance work and explanation to an agency head in order to secure appropriate credentials. Even then, researchers must think through ethical implications of securing entry with authorizations from an agency that may be part of the study. And sometimes, researchers must make judgment calls between locations deemed perfect versus one that is less ideal but acceptable (Erlandson et al. 1993, p. 54). With a quick response scenario, later access might be negotiable.

What researchers should do above all is to identify locations where a "rich mix" of people, relationships, and interactions take place (Marshall and Rossman 1989). Such characteristics do not necessarily imply a location where a lot of people can be found, such as a busy EOC or a large shelter, but where meaningful data can be gathered. Small collections of people can generate remarkable, rich data sources. Lois (2003) studied volunteer search and rescue groups. Though she began her study within the larger organization that supported volunteer groups, she then placed herself (with training) into the teams that went out on rescues. There, she found insights into how team members managed the difficult emotional work of search and rescue.

So how do qualitative disaster researchers find good sites? Doing so begins with knowing the field under study, including the organizations and agencies, the roles, critical processes, and locations-for-action. Too many times, disasters spark the curiosity of people new to the field who rush in without understanding the operational context of fire and emergency management. These "instant experts" then lay claim to critical insights, open consultancies, and fail to contribute to the body of knowledge well established through decades of QDR.

Such newcomers do not include students, who can and should seek out formal mentoring relationships with established disaster researchers. Faculty members can help secure funding, expedite entrée, and guide the student to making a meaningful contribution to science and practice. Their understanding of the body of knowledge can direct the student to help address gaps in knowledge. Their experience with disaster field research methods can point a student to potentially rich sites and, with their existing networks, connect the student to the right people to interview. Faculty members and mentors in the field can also aid students in learning the confusing jargon of the field. Terminology or language is a critical foundation for any culture, and the same is true of disasters. Researchers need to be able to understand the jargon (often used as acronyms: EOC, ICS, NIMS, USAR, AAR, SitRep, FCO[1]) to help conversations flow with minimal time for explanations—especially in a quick response environment.

Regardless of the time frame for QDR, researchers should maintain their focus on promising social situations where places, actors and activities occur (Spradley 1980). One strategy is to look for *kinds* of places: kinds of shelters (public, private, faith-based); kinds of recovery meetings (workshops, planning charettes, committee settings); or kinds of EOCs (fixed, mobile, virtual). The variety of status social actors take on should be considered as well. People assume varying statuses (a position in society) in

---

1 Emergency Operations Center, Incident Command System, National Incident Management System, After Action Report, Situation Report, Federal Coordinating Officer.

social settings: within the shelter (manager, volunteer, resident), recovery meetings (task leader, elected official, citizen, survivor, planner), or EOC (emergency manager, health official, mass care specialist, public information officer).

Statuses are embedded within social relationships and social organizations which can also be considered. Dynes (1970) devised a typology of organizations operating in disasters. The four types reveal the kinds of actors within them. Established organizations like the local emergency management agency may include a director, associate director, public information officer (PIO), social media officer, planner, and others depending on agency size and funding. Expanding organizations, like the Red Cross, increase and decrease in size to meet needs with both paid staff and an extensive set of volunteers. Extending organizations provide resources not traditionally tied to disaster response and recovery. For example, a construction company or a farmer might drive bulldozers to a wildfire site to cut firebreaks around houses. Emergent organizations usually appear to address unmet needs. In 1992, the organization Women Will Rebuild Miami emerged after the predominantly male organization failed to address Hurricane Andrew-related needs for child care, teenagers, and single mothers (Enarson and Morrow 1997).

Spradley (1980) also recommends that researchers seek out sites that involve social activities. Recovery meetings might involve collecting information, informing citizens, soliciting input, developing plans, and securing funding. Efforts might take place at city hall, in stricken neighborhoods, over social media, or through electronic town halls. Spradley advises us to look for social situations with similar activities. To understand shelter behavior might require going to the full range of shelters from those opened officially by the Red Cross to those operated by faith-based organizations without prior shelter training. Those who seek to understand debris management might look for the full range of sites necessary for debris removal: homeowners who sort debris; hazardous materials crews who look for related problems; operators who transform green waste through grinders and chippers into re-usable mulch; incinerators who manage facilities that eliminate waste without compromising air quality; and store owners that salvage and resell usable cupboards, windows, and other construction resources.

Disaster "Zones"

Experts usually advise those looking for sites to start with an accessible social setting (Spradley 1980). Sites must include frequently recurring activities that can be observable and shed insight on the research question. People and places should be selected based on standardized approaches within social science methodology but with an eye to the particular challenges of QDR. For disasters, *spatial zones* should be considered when selecting sites or sampling (Killian 2002). Several types of spatial zones can be discerned. For example, the *impact zone* is an obvious point of interest though discerning the location may be challenging. The epicenter of an earthquake, for example, might not be the place where the most damage occurs. In 2011, for example, the earthquake that triggered the Japanese tsunami occurred offshore. Catastrophic loss of life occurred along the coastline. Continuing problems with the Fukushima-Dai-ichi nuclear plant presented yet another impact zone. As debris drifted eastward, marine traffic, islands, and the western coast of North America braced for potential impacts.

Beyond where researchers locate the impact zone, a *filter zone* can be identified where movement of resources and personnel occurs such as evacuation centers and triage sites. Beyond the filter zone, other defined areas can be found including shelters and recovery centers.

The research methodology must be considered as well when selecting a location. Researchers wanting to conduct observational studies, for example, will need a site which allows for extensive access and the potential to participate in the setting. The observational researcher will need to be able to move around freely in the setting or, at the very least, to have an unobtrusive yet advantageous place from which to conduct observations. Interview locations require places where people can hear each other and information can be recorded. Document collection can vary significantly across settings, with emergent, impact zone, and other ephemeral locations compromising abilities to secure such data. And researchers must be ethically sensitive to the use of any visual data collection sites which may—while seeming to be public—actually contain highly personal sites of social interaction.

Time and Events

Some additional techniques may be especially useful for disaster research, including strategies that pertain to time and events (Burgess 1982b; Schatzman and Strauss 1973). "Functional time" focuses on the phases of an event, such as the warning time period, followed by the impact (a tornado hits a community) and then by the post-impact period when response-related activities like search and rescue occur (Killian 2002). Activities within these times will vary, such as the day versus the night shift. Shelters that serve individuals with medical conditions, for example, staff their facilities with fewer people at night than during the day. Firefighters, who often work 24 hour shifts, observe that the time of day or night results in differing numbers and kinds of calls. The time of the week matters as well for emergency responders, with more domestic violence and suicide calls occurring on the weekends and around the holidays.

The lifetime of an event should also be considered. For example, within the life span of a disaster recovery, it can be possible to discern how people move into temporary housing, the number of temporary locations they stay in, and the time span they need to secure permanent housing. Vulnerability theorists have uncovered differential outcomes by monitoring that time span, noting that low-income families and people with disabilities experience elongated recovery time periods before returning to a permanent location and reacquiring needed medical and social services (Dash, McCoy and Herring 2010; Clive, Davis, Hansen, and Mincin 2010). In short, by attending to time elements in a given setting, researchers can capture the rhythm of the setting, how a typical day unfolds or a process evolves (Neal, in press).

Events

Events should also be sampled (Schatzman and Strauss 1973), a particularly useful technique for disaster sampling. Three types of events might be considered. The first is *routine* events, or moments that occur on a regular basis. Fire departments make runs to car accidents, for example, and EOCs hold annual exercises. The second is a *special* event which is considered fortuitous for the researcher but may be unanticipated. Mitigation planning efforts, for example, occur at irregular times, albeit with an increasing frequency. Being present to examine how that process unfolds offers understanding into community-based interaction, policy-making, and prioritization (Olsen et al. 1998). Probably what interests most disaster researchers, though, are the *untoward* events which include emergency situations.

Other ways to think about events include the magnitude, scope, and size of an event. As described in Chapter 1, disaster researchers conceptualize events along a range from emergency to disaster to catastrophe. After major events like Hurricane Katrina or the Indian Ocean tsunami, researchers produce copious numbers of studies. However, these catastrophic events also appear as statistical outliers with disasters being the far more common event. Researchers need to carefully consider the event in order to permit greater comparison across research studies. Making and implementing recommendations exclusively on the basis of data generated from a single type of event may produce an inappropriate level of preparedness and response.

Finally, consider the kind of event: Is it natural, technological, or human-generated? Some studies have found that blaming erupts when public actors deem a particular actor or agency responsible for the event (Bucher 1957; Blocker and Sherkat 1992). Blaming occurs more commonly in technological (an oil spill, a bridge collapse) or human-generated (anthrax attack, dirty bomb) than in more natural disasters (though not exclusively so). Further, it may be true that psychological reactions to disasters vary depending on the type of event. Does the event intentionally cause harm, such as that inspired by a terrorist event? Or was the event one produced by a misfit between built, physical, and human environments? Or, did the type of event generate concern against an external threat? Did the event result in a "therapeutic" community developing, or a "corrosive" community? Attention to events, settings, people, and time is required to develop a sound research design for QDR.

Methods

Methods include strategies for gathering meaningful data. This section thus focuses on the more commonly-used strategies in QDR: interviews, observations, documents, and visual research.

Interviews

Interviewing represents the most used method in qualitative disaster research. Numerous examples can be found at the major research center websites or journals identified in Chapter 1. Many interviews conducted for disaster studies take place under unique conditions: standing in a tent city under construction while army helicopters carry in loads of plywood, walking on the beach with survivors from a tsunami, sitting on the floor of a public facility sheltering thousands of people, or scrunched into an evacuee's temporary travel trailer while kids run in and out. Indeed, if one thing is certain, it is that most interviews under disaster conditions—sometimes even for years afterward—do not take place in convenient, comfortable, or easy-to-find locations. Conditions vary because disasters disrupt and disable normal routines. In major events, outside organizations arrive to help and set up temporary headquarters in vacant buildings or create tent cities. Even these experienced disaster organizations may have to muck out the flooded facility, build their own bunk beds, and find places to eat. Beyond the response time, it may be difficult to find interviewees, especially for a longitudinal study.

In a major disaster, people may move six or more times. Relocating them can be completely impossible. Older interviewees may have died, gone into nursing homes, or developed medical conditions that impede interviewing (e.g., dementia). Other time periods, such as preparedness and mitigation may prove more accessible and predictable. But even with mitigation there can be challenges. For example, required, post-flooding home elevations along the U.S. Gulf Coast meant that some senior citizens and some people with disabilities could not move home again. Understanding the impact of such mitigation measures became difficult because it was nearly impossible to find people permanently displaced by the elevations. Finding interviewees after a disaster often becomes an exercise in determination and stamina. One may need to go to multi-family complexes known to house evacuees, or post notices inviting participation, or use word of mouth to recruit interviewees (see multiple examples in Weber and Peek, 2013).

Consequently, following the usual rules for conducting an interview may be challenging. One strategy is clear, though: when helicopters buzz overhead or chain saws cut through debris, take careful notes because any recorder is likely to be useless. This section reviews general guidelines for conducting interviews along with suggestions and examples of how to manage conditions that threaten to undermine traditional approaches to conducting a qualitative interview.

The goal of a qualitative interview is the same as qualitative research in general: to capture a full, detailed report full of richness, depth, and breadth. The interview moves respondents and researchers beyond the straightforward "yes or no"-type questions often found on a survey to reveal the full set of considerations someone makes when thinking through a question. Interviews also allow researchers to follow meaningful threads offered by respondents that typically produce moving accounts of lived experiences. On a survey, someone living in a temporary trailer may select "how satisfied" they are on a scale from 1 to 5. But to hear a mother describe her life as "spam in a can" reveals a more visceral account of how she struggles to care for children lacking space to play, interact, or study. Listening to a survivor of domestic violence explain how she cannot protect herself in such a closed location enables researchers to raise awareness among first responders and emergency managers. The depth of understanding gained allows us to make useful recommendations that change policies and procedures—and save lives even well after the disaster has passed.

Conducting an Interview

Traditional qualitative interviews can be described as a conversational partnership in which researchers and interviewees work together to produce meaningful information (Weiss 1994; Rubin and Rubin 2012). Such information sheds light into the emic perspective, and reveals subjective, lived experiences of those under study. And, although the researcher is to work *with* the interviewee, the most important rule to follow is: listen. Stop talking, and allow the interviewee time to answer fully, to reflect deeply, and to generate richer insights. Interviews differ from surveys, where the researcher intervenes to move on to the next question. Instead, traditional qualitative interviews permit and encourage interviewees to offer more fully developed and context-laden responses.

Despite the seeming chaotic nature of response-time period research, certain steps should be considered and employed when undertaking qualitative interviews. A review of these steps is followed by some additional detailed information on key areas.

- *Create Questions.* Interview questions can come from the extant literature, from careful listening to initial respondents, from advisors and colleagues, and from intellectual curiosity (see upcoming section for more detail).
- *Select a Setting.* Choosing where one will conduct an interview can be challenging. Usually, we rely on interviewees to tell us where they would be comfortable, but encourage them to select a location where few interruptions will occur. The non-response phases generally offer more latitude in this, so being ready to conduct an interview in less than ideal conditions is necessary.
- *Set up an Appointment.* Generally, we prefer to set up interviews in advance and always at the convenience of the interviewee. It is polite to confirm the interview time and place in advance, and a formal letter outlining procedures is a good idea. Disaster response time research, again, may involve the researcher in catching interviewees when and where they may be available, so being ready to do any interview at any time is advisable.
- *Conduct the Consent Process.* IRB rules and regulations must be adhered to. Before initiating the interview or turning on a recorder, explain procedures, risks, and benefits, and obtain written consent.
- *Guide the Interview.* Using the checklist (described below), walk the interviewee through telling their story. Do not dominate or cut off an interviewee as doing so will disrupt the conversational flow and discourage the participant from fully disclosing detailed information (see below).
- *Listen and Take Careful Notes.* Probably the most challenging aspect of conducting an interview is managing the process of listening, checking off questions, mentally assessing the completeness of the response, thinking through the next logical question or probe to ask, and taking notes on the verbal and non-verbal

content of the interview. Doing so is mentally and
physically exhausting and is a skill developed over time.
- *Organize and Summarize.* As soon as possible, write up
a summary of the interview. Use the checklist interview
guide to organize the responses as the interviewee may
have digressed. Secure the data under lock and key and
password protect on any computer or device.
- *Transcribe.* As soon as possible, transcribe the interview
fully and carefully. Consider sending the transcript back
to the interviewee to check for accuracy.
- *Code.* As soon as possible, conduct an initial coding
of the data and revisit the interview guide. Determine
what the codes mean for the future of the project, for the
interview guide, and for which persons to invite as the
next interviewees.

Developing the Interview Guide. The research question drives the
interview questions, which should be sorted and organized into thematic content areas. At first, "puzzlements and jottings" (Lofland
et al. 2006) serve as a basis for what might end up in an interview
guide. Efforts also usually involve searching the literature for good
ideas, in part so that we do not reinvent the wheel and do help push
forward the body of knowledge. Observations from field sites may
also produce ideas on what to ask. Participant observation inside a
Community Emergency Response Team might guide a researcher in
asking questions about formal and informal hierarchies, the availability of resources, and inter-organizational relationships. Documents
might indicate areas of inquiry, for example, a mitigation policy on
elevations might focus inquiry on which actors were involved in
determining floodplains and storm surge, creating related building codes, and conducting inspections to determine compliance.
Suggestions by colleagues and potential respondents also help to
produce possible questions. Or, one might proceed by looking at a
known process, such as the steps in a warning (Mileti 1999).

For example, a study on how people learned about warnings
might ask people how they first learned of the warning, what they
did upon receiving the warning, with whom they may have interacted, and the time frame between warning receipt and taking
action. It makes sense to order these steps chronologically, and
to include sub-steps as possible probes in each. For example, one

might listen carefully for all forms of warning receipt and, if the interviewee does not mention them, ask about specific transmission mechanisms: television, radio, social media, sirens, smart phone apps, or "other."

The basic rules of developing good questions apply here (see Table 2.4). Words familiar to respondents should be used and researchers should avoid jargon, or assuming that people understand acronyms (e.g., FEMA, ICS, NIMS). Good qualitative questions avoid yes/no replies, in an effort to encourage respondents to tell their story with depth and breadth. For example, asking "did you receive any warning" will produce a yes/no answer while "tell me how you first learned about the wildfire" will likely produce a fuller description. Regardless, asking a good first question is key and can either inspire or deter a participant (see Table 2.4).

Table 2.4

Developing Good Questions

Question Issue	Poorly Worded	Better
A good opening question	How many people work in your agency? Did people evacuate?	Tell me about the kinds of people who work here. Describe what people did after the explosion.
Ask questions they can answer	Was the tornado an EF4 or an EF5?	Can you tell me about the kinds of damage that you observed after the tornado?
Multi-barreled (look for "and" or "or").	Tell me how you opened the EOC *and* brought in the staff?	Tell me how you opened the EOC? (*Later*: How did you bring in the staff despite the storm?)
Yes/No questions	Did you distribute brochures about debris removal procedures?	How did you inform people about how to remove debris from their properties? (*Probe*: types of informational materials).

(*continued*)

Table 2.4 (Continued)		
Question Issue	Poorly Worded	Better
Leading questions	Shouldn't case managers be formally trained to help disaster survivors?	How do you think case managers should be prepared to help disaster survivors?
Straightforward and simple	Given that the storm moved across multiple jurisdictions, wouldn't it have been a good idea to establish formal MOU's, conduct pre-planning and exercises?	How did you manage an event that went outside of your jurisdiction? To what extent were those actions pre-arranged?
Avoid jargon (depending on who you are talking to; some expertise may be relevant)	When did the na-tech develop?	Can you tell me when the flood waters entered the nuclear plant?
Based in part on Babbie, 2010; Gorden 1992.		

Pilot tests of the initial interview guide may reveal additional aspects to include. Likewise, careful analysis of the first interview(s) may lead the researcher to additional items to include such as a specific local weather application or the role of family and friends. A naturalistic perspective allows the researcher to incorporate new findings and to develop and re-develop the interview instrument in an effort to hone in on critical information. Developing the instrument as a checklist is also a good idea, as participants may not go in chronological order (Richardson 1987). Someone may learn of the warning, take shelter immediately, and then check an app or call a friend—or they may leave safe shelter to return for a pet or neighbor.

Guiding the Interview. By listening actively, researchers can check off the relevant content while allowing the interviewee to tell their story. Listening is a skill. Several obstacles may threaten active listening: noise, intrusions, settings, fatigue, and experience. In addition, semantic obstacles may prevent good listening (Gorden 1992). We all come from social class levels that influence how we speak, regions and cultures that influence what we say, and professions/educational levels that effect the way in which we verbally interact. We should be mindful of such influences on listening, as people may use words and phrases that mean something to them but not to us, and vice versa. Active listening means that we pay attention to people's words in a larger context while we consider their words vis-à-vis the intent of our instrument: Are we hearing information that sheds light on our research question?

Researchers actively encourage interviewees both verbally and non-verbally (head nods, smiles of encouragement) to continue (Gorden 1992). Attempts should be made to manage intrusions (Weiss 1994). Motivate participants by helping them to place themselves into the moment under discussion. Offer time cues: "So after the levees broke, what were your first actions?" or "Can you take me back to the first mitigation planning meeting?" Interviewers should always avoid using argumentative language or loaded words: "Why are you mad at FEMA?" Rather, "How does that make you feel?" reflects more neutral language (Gorden 1992). Ask respondents to illustrate: "Can you give me an example of how you distributed the preparedness kit information?"

Skilled interviewers can also observe non-verbally. It may be easy to see if someone's eyes glisten with tears as they movingly describe the influence of volunteers on their lives or the loss of a beloved pet. Seeing goosebumps on someone's arm as they talk about the sounds of the tornado should also be recorded. With experience and further study, good researchers will also pay attention to and record body language (tense or relaxed), posture (ambivalent or engaged), tone of voice (eager or bored), and eye movement (eye contact or avoidance). Active listening, coupled with skilled observation, can similarly divulge what people offer or do not offer: Do they talk about losses or avoid them? Do they seem angered by certain questions and stop talking on the subject under discussion? Attending to non-verbal comment matters and should be incorporated into notes as a supplement to the transcript. For example, someone who says "FEMA is terrific!" on a transcript may actually have rolled their eyes and used a tone of sarcasm—or the reverse. Good note-taking on non-verbal material helps you to interpret what people really mean. Active listening and observing matters, because guiding an interview can be quite complex.

Interviewees rarely follow your carefully crafted interview guide. They know their story as they know it—not in the organized, perhaps chronologically laid-out way that you developed, sorted, and categorized your interview questions. Good qualitative researchers allow interviewees to tell their story as they listen, observe, and check off the interview questions. Guiding the participant through the process means just that: moving them gently through the conversation (rather than a jackhammer inquisition) to produce meaningful, rich detail. True, you may need to wade through some less useful information (and possibly transcribe it), but interrupting your respondent usually stops their flow of thought and, often, their willingness to reveal their backstage behavior.

Keeping interviewees on track, then, means constantly assessing where they were, where you are, and where you need to go. Interviewers will need to redirect politely any interviewee who strays. Whyte (1955) says that we can do so using temporal clues (see Figure 2.1).

Redirecting people can be as simple as probing on a particular detail: "Could you tell me more about how people arranged their cots in the shelter?" Both verbal and silent probes (counting to ten while giving time to respond) can be used to encourage more depth. You might also redirect someone to an idea from earlier, which is not part of the topic at hand: "I want to go back to an earlier comment you made, that convincing people of the importance of mitigation is challenging. Could you tell me more about how you did convince people?" The most significant change of direction occurs when you introduce a new topic. One should always alert the interviewee that this is about to happen: "Thank you for tell me about removing the debris from the slab. Let's talk now about how you went about securing a building contractor." Throughout it all, researchers should guide, motivate, verbally and non-verbally affirm the respondent's information, and—always—listen. Take time to verbally reward participants for sharing their

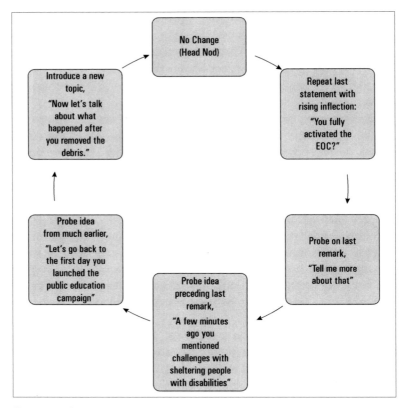

Figure 2.1 Changing direction (based on Whyte 1955; Gorden 1992; Weiss 1994)

lives, experiences, and opinions for your project and always be sure to send a handwritten thank you note. Remember, you must leave the door open for the next researcher to enter.

Focus Groups

Focus groups represent an efficient, though sometimes challenging, way to gather qualitative data through group interviews. To conduct a focus group, researchers invite appropriate individuals to a common location for a moderated group discussion. By definition (Krueger and Casey 2000), focus groups rely on a semi-structured set of questions. Facilitators invite participants to respond openly, guiding the discussion on relevant questions to elicit useful information from all participants. By inviting people to join in a group setting, data can be gathered efficiently and expeditiously. However, the process is not without some challenges. Facilitators or moderators must be skilled in group interaction skills, able to discern levels of participation among those present, manage overly verbose attendees, and decrease inhibitions among more reticent individuals. Effective facilitators acknowledge and facilitate the flow of personalities in a dynamic group setting and direct the focus group toward productive results. Clearly, organizing and managing focus groups takes considerable personal skills and high levels of concentration.

Managing the size of the group helps. Peek and Fothergill (2009) found that a group size of 3 to 5 worked best, observing that larger groups tended to inhibit fuller participation of more quiet individuals. Researchers select participants based on the purpose of the research, and find them through word of mouth, e-mail solicitations, advertisements, flyers, and by extending formal invitations through organizations, agencies, and associations. Peek and Fothergill (2009) recommend recruiting actively to find and involve key stakeholders. In their research on the experiences of Muslim Americans after September 11th, e-mail and flyers posted through a Muslim Student Association enabled them to find focus group participants. People may spontaneously ask to join as they learn about the study (Krueger and Casey 2000). Spontaneous participation occurred when teachers asked to join focus groups after Peek and Fothergill (2009) launched research on the effects of Hurricane Katrina on children. Their research included groups with children aged three to nine, middle school students, elementary education teachers, and mothers.

Structuring the group and the setting is always wise, though not always possible in terms of ideal set ups. A convenient and comfortable location for the participants—even a familiar one—should be selected. Care must be taken to insure confidentiality within the group and that human subjects feel respected and safe. The researcher must decide how to record the content (audio, video, or both, or through note-taking, including verbal and non-verbal behavior) in a manner that feels acceptable to participants. The facilitator first explains the purpose of the study, the benefits and potential risks, and the manner in which their information will be safeguarded (Krueger and Casey 2000). Facilitators should then acknowledge that everyone's point of view is vital and work to elicit perspectives from all present. Questions can proceed from semi-structured to unstructured questions as deemed appropriate for the purpose of the study, the type of participants present, and their cultural preferences for interaction. Food or other benefits may be provided to participants, such as information on wildfires, how to help children with disasters, or even gift cards for gasoline, bus fare, or food.

The goal of a focus group is to elicit information focused on a topic at hand. In one study (Roberts et al. 2004), researchers spoke with groups of adults given a free smoke alarm in London. Their research included a diverse set of participants, revealing the necessity of speaking locally relevant languages and understanding people's cultures. For example, researchers carefully stratified the study to insure that high risk groups (households with children or seniors) were included, and that people representing all five types of smoke alarms participated. Given that 23% of the study participants did not speak English, group participants had the option of using an interpreter. To increase further people's comfort, focus groups met at a local community center. Researchers felt that they reached their goal when "saturation" occurred and they kept hearing the same thing: that false alarms were so irritating people disconnected their detectors. Others refused installation, not wanting strangers to enter their homes. Results indicated that new designs should be considered along with continued education over the proper use, maintenance, and replacement of detectors.

An effort in Houston, Texas further demonstrates the importance of language and culture (Nepal et al. 2010). Concerned over lack of disaster preparedness among recent immigrants, researchers used 2000 U.S. census data to identify spatial clusters of recent immigrants speaking Spanish, Chinese, Vietnamese, and Somali. Linguistically isolated with limited English proficiency and few English speakers in the household, researchers brought in native speakers for focus groups. They recruited through community-based organizations and multicultural agencies by posting flyers in area stores, agencies, work sites, and other community locations. To aid in connecting with the communities, researchers recruited and trained local community leaders to help with recruiting and convening focus groups, which they held at local agencies, churches, and apartment buildings. Even so, participants feared joining in because of the study's association with a government agency. Nepal et al. (2010, p. 57) note that:

"Conducting participatory research with linguistically isolated populations demands not only considerable linguistic fluency, but also cultural skills pertinent to the respective native language group, nationality, and ethnicity of the participants. In general, it is rare that a researcher will be both multilingual and multicultural." To address these challenges, they used two well-trained facilitators per focus group. Even so, researchers realized that social, economic, and educational differences between participants and facilitators may have impeded culturally and linguistically based understanding as well as group dynamics.

Peek and Fothergill (2009) further recommend that researchers acknowledge diversity within a focus group, which can be addressed through careful advance research of the population along with intentionally stratifying the sample. For example, their study of Muslims necessarily incorporated the diverse set of beliefs and practices across Islam. In addition, they needed to recognize and understand that gender roles influence who speaks, how much, and when. Focus groups can be particularly valuable for gaining entrée to vulnerable or stigmatized groups, as evidenced by the studies reported in this section (Peek and Fothergill 2009).

Observation

Observation can be conducted in several ways, including the researcher's role and the extent to which the technique is used. First, the researcher's role can fall along a continuum from complete observer to complete participant. Each role offers insights and problems. From the stance of the complete observer, it may be difficult to discern what the fire chief is thinking when making her decision about how to manage arriving vehicles, establish incident command, assign personnel, or fight the fire. Assuming what the fire chief thinks is fraught with potential error—but does insure that the researcher is not in the way or become injured. Conversely, being a full participant observer (working on a fire crew) may elicit deeper and richer understanding (Desmond 2009; Lois 2003). However, as a researcher moves along the continuum from observer to participant, the potential to influence the actions of subjects increases. Such influence may mean that other participants hide their real feelings or find ways to divert the researcher from what is really going on. The researcher may also sway the actions of the subject(s). Choices regarding the role of the researcher must be made along with the potential consequences (positive and negative) of taking on the observation role. Ideally, observation will be triangulated with another qualitative data technique, such as interviews with fire chiefs or emergency managers—and/or with the use of emergency operations plans and after-action reports.

Due to the closed nature of much of the first responder, emergency management, and homeland security communities, it may take considerable effort for a researcher to gain entrée, move past gatekeepers, establish rapport, and begin collecting data. Richard Rotanz (2006), an emergency manager from New York City, recommends that researchers develop relationships prior to studying an event (where possible). He sees benefits (Rotanz 2006, p. 474): "Let's start here, in our university offices and from our emergency operation centers, and pick up the phone. A simple introduction of each other will lead to a long-term relationship..." Researchers may need to go even further, securing official letters that enable them to move past barricades. Some topics and locations remain elusive, however. Even with funding from one's top scientific agency, it may not be possible to move into shelters, hospitals, morgues, or temporary trailer parks and relief camps. Each setting will likely require careful negotiation for entrée, with persistent and patient efforts to secure data.

The second major choice that must be made concerns the general approach and use of observation techniques. Observation may occur in a fairly straightforward manner where a researcher merely sits and records what can be seen, probably using a checklist that directs attention to specific research questions. For example, imagine attending a recovery task force meeting after a major disaster. A straightforward research question might be: "What is the composition of the task force committee?" The researcher will then note relevant dimensions regarding that composition— such as the occupations of people who are present, along with gender, age, race, or ethnicity, neighborhoods, and other relevant demographics. The researcher might then move on to ask: "Who influences the recovery task force and in what ways?" by marking next to each person's name every time the person speaks and the amount of time they speak. Careful analysis of field notes or recordings can systematically reveal the general theme of their comments. Over time, it will be possible to identify the paths ultimately taken by the recovery task force and to trace those paths back to the original influences. After Hurricane Andrew, for example, women felt they were being excluded from the major recovery task force (We Will Rebuild) and formed their own (Women Will Rebuild). The women's lobbying efforts ultimately increased funding and attention to issues surrounding child care, concerns with teens, and domestic violence (Enarson and Morrow 1997). The majority of disaster research seems to be of such an effort—observation in a limited time fashion and supplemented with interviews and document analysis. A far different observation effort, ethnography, offers an even richer set of insights into emergencies and disasters. Ethnography can be defined as an in-depth study of people in their native context. Ethnographic records require the researcher to investigate the culture of the people or organization under study. Anthropologists are among those most likely to use extended ethnographic techniques. In 2013, anthropologist Anthony Oliver-Smith received the Malinowski Award from the Society for Applied Anthropology. Oliver-Smith has studied indigenous displacement from disasters, examining the ways in which people experience loss and resettlement. His work has inspired others to look at the role of culture in response and recovery from catastrophic events worldwide (e.g., Oliver-Smith 1986; Hoffman and Oliver-Smith 2002; Oliver-Smith 2009).

To produce culturally-rich findings, Spradley (1980) created the Developmental Research Sequence, a series of steps that guide researchers to hone in on culture through observational strategies. In short, the steps move the researcher from locating a potentially fruitful social situation, conducting participatory observation, making careful notes through extensive descriptions, and then moving into a series of increasingly sophisticated analyses (domain, taxonomic, and componential, see below). The goal is to uncover cultural themes that move readers into the lived experiences of wildland firefighters, emergency operations centers, or long-term volunteer crews. A good ethnography takes readers inside the culture, reveals insider perspectives, and explains the culture theoretically.

Key to all techniques is taking good notes. Traditionally, three ways to take notes can be used. The first is mental notes, which means that you have to remember key elements of the observation encounter: who was there, how many were there, a physical description of the event/location, and the general flow of events (Lofland et al. 2006). Obviously, mental notes can easily fail as time passes—so develop these mental records into written materials immediately. A second technique, jotted notes, can be taken fairly inconspicuously. Jotted notes include key phrases, words and quotes designed to jog the researcher's memory when crafting fuller notes. Mental and jotted notes, while not ideal, may be particularly necessary in emergencies and disasters as you really do not want to open your laptop to record data when the earth is moving, the tsunami has been announced, or the tornado is bearing down. Doing so might also unduly influence those under study as some devices may be too conspicuous. Moving to a location where mental or jotted notes can be transferred to fuller notes is essential, though. As a rule, never sleep before writing up your field notes and be sure to schedule time to do so. Full field notes expand on the mental and jotted notes. Several techniques can be used to develop full notes.

The first technique, known as the "C-Model" was developed at the Disaster Research Center. Though the number and type of "C's" have varied over the years, four tend to remain: characteristics, chronology, conditions, and consequences (Quarantelli 2002). Imagine, for example, a field report that is organized into each of these sections. You might find the following (see a fuller development below):

- *Characteristics.* What are the features of the individual, organization or community?
- *Chronology.* How did the event or process unfold over time?
- *Conditions.* What pre-existing contexts produced physical and social vulnerability? What kinds of social, economic, environmental, or political factors influenced how the event unfolded? How did such factors impact the outcomes?
- *Consequences.* What are the obvious and less obvious outcomes of the event, interactions, processes, or decisions?

A second technique useful for producing fuller sets of field notes comes from Spradley (1980) who offers several field note principles and techniques. Field note principles include ensuring that you identify the speaker in your notes so that you can clearly follow who said what and when they said it. Distinguishing between human subjects (natives) and yourself is particularly important to do. Spradley also recommends the "verbatim principle" where the researcher records comments exactly as they are made, word-for-word. A final "concrete principle" advises the researcher to create field notes using concrete words—this is not the time to write the next great Pulitzer Prize winning novel. The researcher should include just the facts in words as clear as possible: who, what, when (Lofland et al. 2006).

Often, new researchers find it difficult to know what to focus on. Spradley again guides us to specific foci: the spaces that people use, the people who are in them, and the activities they do, the objects or physical items present in the setting, individual and interactive acts, events that occur, what happens over time, the goals of those present, and the feelings that can be observed. Imagine, for example, conducting observations in a temporary relief camp. How do people organize their tents? What objects can be found in and around the tents? Who does what during a typical day? How are meals arranged? Who interacts with whom to insure personal safety (Williams 1992)? What do people think about the structure and resources of the camp?

A final useful strategy from Spradley guides researchers in making grand and mini-tours of the scene. A mini-tour focuses on a small portion of a setting, such as the desk of the logistics officer in the EOC or the children's aisle of a donations management warehouse. A grand tour broadens the mental image by moving to the full layout of desks in the EOC or the entire warehouse with donations for all ages and needs. The mini-tour allows researchers to understand better the micro-level of an organizational configuration and how an individual manages a specific task. The grand tour takes a step back to see activities in a larger context. The full set of ESFs may be viewed in their relation to logistics, for example. Or, it may be possible to now see that donations for children represent the single largest items managed in the warehouse.

Unobtrusive Measures

As defined, unobtrusive measures (also referred to as "nonreactive" measures) include tangible items or traces that people have created or left behind (Webb et al. 1981). The majority of such items include documents such as those found in archives (letters, diaries, reports, newspapers, see Hill 1993). Unobtrusive measures can also mean items created in the context of a disaster such as debris (destroyed buildings or piles of used materials at a shelter), signs (hand-made or professionally produced), or even quilts, public art, and memorials. Many fields use such data—forensic scientists, for example, as well as arson investigators, police detectives, the FBI and Homeland Security. In disaster research, unobtrusive measures represent underused data sources as primary data. However, as part of a research design that triangulates data, disaster researchers rely heavily on documents, reports, memos, and similar materials.

Documents

Documents can be defined as sources that shed light into individual experience and reveals the agency of actors engaged in social interaction (Plummer 1993). A range of documents can be used in research, including public and private records. Public census data, for example, reveal the potential number of socially and/or economically vulnerable populations in a given location. Emergency Operations Plans (EOPs) yield information on inter-organizational coordination (or the lack thereof). Private records also shed insight. After the attacks of September 11th, for example, employee e-mails showed efforts to find co-workers. The National Museum of American History, which is part of the Smithsonian, captured those e-mails for a public exhibit (http://americanhistory.si.edu/september11/collection/collection_index.asp).

Disaster scholars may be particularly interested in episodic records, which capture events that occur sporadically and usually without notice. Despite the unexpectedness, records do exist that can be analyzed. Emergency Operations Centers (EOCs) usually record events in an EOC log, either in writing or virtually. Arson records, 9-1-1 dispatcher call logs, safety reviews (such as FAA inspection records), after action reports, and social media represent a bounty of potential information. Such records can be used to confirm or negate a respondent's perception of events or as a means to jog memories. Increasingly, such episodic records can be retrieved via the Internet. Situation Reports, also called SitReps, can usually be found posted at an Emergency Management

Agency's website. These SitReps record relevant data as the event unfolds, such as the location of damage, numbers of injured, disruptions (and restorations) to infrastructure and utilities, opening and closing of shelters along with the number of residents, sites for donation drop-offs, and other emerging issues.

Physical Traces

Physical traces may also be used as unobtrusive data sources and fall into two types: erosion and accretion (Webb et al. 1999). Erosion refers to the wear and tear of an area after an event. Public shelters, for example, may be overwhelmed by use and even sustain damage—particularly in emergent locations not designed for mass use. Damage to emergency vehicles or the wear and tear on emergency gear also represent erosion data. Collection of respirators and other breathing apparatus after September 11th, for example, could have indicated use, non-use, and the life-span of such gear. Given the continuing health problems of those who responded or assisted with the clean-up, such analysis represents an important first step in longitudinal analysis (Landrigan et al. 2004; Herbert et al. 2006).

Conversely, accretion is defined as what has been added in or left behind. Odometers record the distances traveled during a wildfire. Social media capture initial reactions ("#Earthquake!") as well as serving as early indicators where damage and injuries may have occurred. As the recovery progresses, Facebook, Twitter, and other media reveal patterns of volunteering, the development of unmet needs, or the celebrations associated with businesses re-opening (Crowe 2012; Sutton et al. 2011; Palen 2009; Sutton 2008). In Santa Cruz, California, after the 1989 earthquake, local artists created a Plywood People's Plaza to restore beauty and publicly express concerns in the devastated downtown. Local artists helped children to create a plywood teddy bear, while others built a homeless person pushing a grocery cart. A few years later, nearby Watsonville created a tiled fountain mural depicting the journey of local Hispanics and Anglos. After initial social justice concerns, Hispanics and Anglos worked together and transformed their city into a more inclusive community, celebrated in the mural. Solis et al. (1995) described three types of debris after a disaster, all of which constitute accretion. Debris generated by disaster includes destroyed fences, trees, landscapes, playgrounds, businesses, homes, and infrastructure. Debris generated indirectly includes soil, mud, rocks, sediment, sand, and green matter (trees, leaves) produced by storms, tsunamis, and landslides. Abnormal patterns of life produce rotting food, overly-donated items, water bottles, and other items produced by shelter life, clean-up, and reconstruction.

Unobtrusive measures can be analyzed as an exclusive data source or as part of a triangulated methodology. Enarson (2000), for example, looked at the quilt art produced by survivors dealing with the aftermath of the Red River Valley flood near the U.S. and Canadian border. Enarson relied on quilts as cultural artifacts that could be read like a text. Applying a feminist theoretical lens, Enarson uncovered the role of women's interpersonal networks in quiltmaking and in expressing gendered concerns. Similarly, most researchers examine unobtrusive measures for the trends and patterns revealed in the "data." In addition, content analysis using quantitative measures can be used: the amount of newspaper column space devoted to a topic or the frequency of a word used in political speeches about a disaster. It is appropriate, though, to identify the benefits as well as the issues associated with unobtrusive measures.

Benefits

The benefits of unobtrusive data include the idea that such items do not—to varying degrees—directly involve human subjects and therefore presumably *generate minimal reactions*. Archival records, for example, usually exist because people and organizations have created them. At the Oklahoma City National Memorial and Museum, an extensive archive has been created of numerous items related to the 1995 bombing of the Murrah Federal building in Oklahoma City (http://www.oklahomacitynationalmemorial.org and see the "Collections" section; a Virtual Archive permits viewing of selected items). Available materials range from 9-1-1 calls to pieces of the building and the truck that exploded. Various collections include records and items pertaining to site history, emergency response, public and media response, memorials sent from around the world, the investigation and trials, and the process of creating the memorial. Archivists manage the 4,000 foot, climate-controlled storage unit to protect and preserve over 600,000 items.

These materials form collections critically important to understanding emergency response, terrorism, and recovery. The archive includes deeply meaningful and painful items: toys from the child care center where 19 children died; items linked to those lost and left on the memorial chairs now bearing their names; and thousands of mementos tucked into the wire fence used since April 19, 1995 as an impromptu memorial. The range of materials at the OKC Memorial and Museum demonstrate how "unobtrusive" measures may vary in their impact from deadly serious to deeply painful. Educators, including those interested in viewing these items, can request a "Hope Trunk" exhibit be sent to them for classroom use.

A classic analysis of items left at a different memorial was undertaken by Wagner-Pacifici and Schwartz (1991). Their work examined mementos offered by visitors at the Vietnam Veterans Memorial in Washington D.C. National Park Service staff, who diligently retrieve and store the items, created an archive of the materials. The authors took a careful sample of written messages and items found in the storage facility and identified themes from the data. Their analysis noted that we live in a "culture of commemoration" which helps us to preserve and celebrate our beliefs. The Memorial, and the items left behind, foster group sentiment and unity and even allow us to work through differences and conflict toward common ground. They found that people transformed the Vietnam Veterans Memorial from a place of contemplation into an emotional shrine. Despite the original intent of the memorial, which was designed as an unobtrusive object itself, people transformed the Memorial through leaving messages and mementos.

Other benefits exist as well, particularly the use of unobtrusive measures as a means to *triangulate findings*. Documents or other items can be compared to interview data. For example, a police report may indicate that 60 people were arrested in an area closed to the public after a disaster. The media may then spread a story of 60 people arrested for looting. The report and the story can then be compared to interview data, which reveals that although 60 people were indeed arrested, the charge was not looting—the majority were simply trying to retrieve personal items from their own homes (Fisher 1998). Consider another type of document—the number and kind of donations given in a disaster. Typically, generous donors overwhelm local abilities to manage and process unsolicited items, including used clothing and canned goods (Kendra and Wachtendorf 2001; Neal 1993). Little research has been conducted on the content of such donations. After the May 3, 1999 tornado outbreak across Oklahoma, a collaborative effort between state agencies and voluntary organizations produced a multi-agency warehouse to store massive donations. A local agency, Housing and Urban Development, created a database of donations. Items leaving the warehouse first (which presumably indicated immediate needs) included baby resources (car seats, baby wipes, diapers, formula), beds and bedding, appliances and individual cases of food, towels, juices, cereal, and cleaning supplies. By triangulating with interviews, a donations management process became clear: Items entered the warehouse managed by Seventh Day Adventists, were sorted by Americorps volunteers, inventoried by HUD staff, distributed to organizations identified by the American Red Cross, and picked up directly by survivors at various distribution points (see Figure 2.2).

Unobtrusive measures may also shed insight into more *subjective elements* of the human experience in disasters. Documents and personal items allow us to understand the lived experience of an

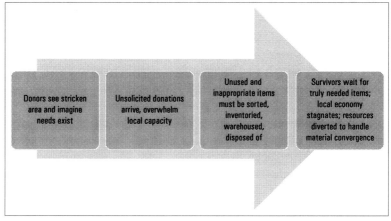

Figure 2.2 The problem of unsolicited donations (From Phillips 2010 with permission)

event, giving us native insights into human behavior. When people share their thoughts and feelings in diaries or letters—or in the art they produce after an event, we can capture the deeper, richer meaning of an event for that individual (Thomas and Znaniecki 1919). A final benefit of unobtrusive data is that they are available, albeit to varying degrees. For researchers and students looking for data useful for theses, dissertations, and research agendas, the availability of unobtrusive data can reduce research costs significantly. Look around in your community or region for archives, libraries, newspaper morgues, and similar sources. You might find an inexpensive and interesting way to conduct research.

Issues

Although not the most commonly used data source within disaster studies, unobtrusive measures can indeed prove valuable if various issues are addressed. Foremost among those issues should be a concern with the ethics of using such data. Determining what is private and what is not is the first step (Webb et al. 1999). Public archives presumably mean open access—but when disaster strikes, sometimes personal items become public. The toys mentioned earlier in the Oklahoma City National Memorial and Museum represent such a conundrum for the researcher: To what extent should we conduct research that might be painful?

Several other types of issues arise with unobtrusive measures, particularly issues of *selective deposit* (Plummer 2001; Webb et al. 1999). Official archives, for example, may not include everything that a researcher truly needs because such items were not donated or collected. They may simply not exist due to the passage of time or out of personal intent. Organizational and public records may not be complete because it is simply difficult to record everything during an emergency and because data (especially that useful to researchers) is not a high priority. More appropriately, human life safety is paramount. Researchers may need to carry on extensive searches to find the information they need, using creative and persistent methods to do so (Scanlon 2002). *Selective retrieval* issues may also arise. You may not always be able to get something, such as records that might be sealed until after someone's death. Or, an archivist might believe they can provide a document or file but find that it has been misplaced or has deteriorated.

Sampling may be a problem, too. Archival records may not always be as amenable to random sampling as that conducted by Wagner-Pacifici and Schwartz (1991) with the Vietnam Veterans Memorial. Records may be incomplete, which introduces sampling issues. For example, when studying a voluntary organization, project leaders may not have had time to manage dozens of volunteers and also submit weekly reports. To try and sample from existing records, then, you must take incompleteness into account. Public shelters opened for a disaster are notorious for incomplete records, preferring to spend their time feeding people and providing basic amenities. Completing paperwork is not a high priority.

Researchers should always question the *authenticity* of the document or item. Errors can occur when such items are produced, particularly when a set of office employees contribute to a document—making the author(s) unclear. Another source of error happens when items, donated to an archive, are misidentified by the donor or the archivist. In many cases, documents simply come into collections without the author being known. *Historicity and temporality* matter as well. When was a document created? In what context? Under what circumstances? The *arpilleristas* of Chile, for example, created burlap (*arpillera*) textiles under conditions of extreme political oppression. Seemingly developed to generate income for the poor, the *arpilleristas* graphically embroidered scenes of torture and repression as a means to send protest outside of their limited worlds (Boldt and White 2011).

Finally, researchers themselves may experience tunnel vision and/or fatigue when searching through collections, archives, bins, files, and electronic records. Sometimes, conducting unobtrusive research is a little like looking for the needle in the haystack. You could miss the key item completely because of the volume of documents and materials that have to be searched. Researchers must monitor their attention span and fatigue level in order to reduce missing such items. Determination pays off. In nearly a year of research, I kept searching for a long-missing film made in 1958. Named *El Dorado* after a town in Kansas destroyed by a tornado, the film represented the first moving images of Mennonite Disaster Service (MDS) volunteers. After looking through multiple archives, talking to dozens of volunteers, and writing to many librarians and archivists, I assumed (along with MDS) that the film had been lost to time. On one final research trip, *El Dorado* finally surfaced—when an archivist put in just the right search terms and found the original film can buried in a file folder.

To manage issues associated with documents, start by determining the nature, background, and context of the document. Webb et al. (1999, pp. 163-164) suggest that researchers first determine the history of the document and the means by which it was acquired. Is it truly an original document pertinent to the research question? Is it complete or is there a chance that it is a partial document—or could it have been modified? Are the authors or organization that produced the document identifiable? Why was the document produced, for what purpose? On what is the document based? Is it an original account, a reconstruction, or a second hand version of events? Could the authors have introduced bias (intentionally or not) into the content? How open were the authors in presenting the content? Finally, to develop further credibility, are there any other documents that provide insights on the event or topic or substantiate the document in hand?

Kreps (1994) dug into archives in the Disaster Research Center. DRC personnel spent eleven years from 1963 to 1974 transcribing interviews for ongoing studies and for placement into the archives. Each transcription was then inventoried and linked to various documents for a range of disaster events. Kreps spent years reading through hundreds of the transcriptions to develop a structural code about organization and collective behavior. His study investigated 1,062 transcriptions and documents revealing 423 instances of collective organization. Though he found the archives to be somewhat uneven and some of the studies to be exploratory (which is not uncommon in quick response research), a number of rich, detailed cases were uncovered. Kreps noted that "my feelings about the overall value of the DRC data archives and field research methods that generated them are very positive. There have been important theoretical and practical yields from DRC research, and a large number of people have received sociological training in the process" (Kreps 1994, p. 70). Kreps' experience in the DRC archives is consistent with what you may experience as well. Despite the challenges of using unobtrusive measures and archives, significant advances in theory and research can be generated.

Visual Research Methodology

From 1896 to 1916, the *American Journal of Sociology* (volumes 2–12) included photos. The photos provided emic perspectives of saloons, municipal playgrounds, Appalachia, and the Chicago stockyards (Stasz 1979). Of those visual researchers, half were women who worked in applied settings like the Chicago settlement home founded by Jane Addams named Hull House. A change in editors and policy shifted content toward a more traditional methodology; visual methods disappeared and women's contributions declined dramatically. Visual research would not re-emerge or regain popularity until the 1970s, despite classic anthropological field research by Bateson and Mead (1942) who collected and analyzed 25,000 photos to reveal Balinese child-rearing practices (Wagner 1979; Harper 1998). Visual research regained popularity in the 1960s when Worth and Adair (1970) put cameras into the hands of Navajos; Thompson, Clarke and Dinitz (1974) studied the impact of Vietnam war images; and Goffman (1979) questioned gendered advertising images. Use of visual methods spread across disciplines with archaeology using visual images to map and record spatial relationships, health professions using visual data for comparative studies, and botany using images to measure growth. Techniques using videotapes, still photographs, digital images, web images, and camera phones have progressed steadily across the past few decades (Becker 1975, 1978, 1981;Curry and Clarke 1977; Gottdiener 1979; Albrecht 1985; Blinn 1987; Ball and Smith 1992; Hockings 1995).

Disaster researchers have largely failed to incorporate visual methods into their work, despite its clear value. Today, a range of digital tools provide still and moving images of interest to researchers and practitioners. Given that visual images provide practical value for arson investigation, homeland security, and disaster damage assessments, the use of visual methods should be encouraged, albeit with a rigorous methodological approach and a strong ethical stance. The arrival of these methods has been accompanied with new journals (e.g., *Journal of Visual Culture, Visual Studies*) and guidance to inform a more systematic approach to using visual images. This section thus focuses on reasons to use visual data, thinking visually, developing visual literacy, types of visual images, data-gathering and sampling, and processes for analyzing visual data.

Social scientists have become engaged in the use of visual data because of the content that, once analyzed, can reveal meaningful social relationships and social complexity. Wagner (1979) argues that photographs can be used to stimulate interviews, to record social phenomena systematically, and to reveal emic perspectives. Indeed, those who generate visual images often do so as a means to record moments in time that may even be iconic in nature (Grady 1996). Iconic communications communicate information (see Figure 2.3 of wheelchair sign on bridge). Careful examination of visual images can yield theoretical insights as well.

Thinking Visually

Working with visual data requires that we develop an ability to think visually. By developing visual literacy, we acquire an understanding that a photo is a nonlinear form of communication and that we can actively question the image, its meaning and its context. Collier and Collier (1986) argue that two key elements must be present in a photograph for potential research use. First, it must provide cultural elements so that details can be seen in a context. A parallel would be to take a sentence from an interview out of

Figure 2.3 A need for help reflected in handmade signs left on a New Orleans bridge after Hurricane Katrina.
Photo courtesy of Pam Jenkins and Barbara Davidson.

its context– the meaning could be lost, transformed or misunderstood. Lacking a context, additional information is often needed to interpret the images that are captured. To illustrate, a series of photos that show donated items leaving a local church and into the hands of survivors may suggest that such donations are needed— when in reality unsolicited donations tend to overwhelm local areas, particularly canned goods and used clothing. A second key element is that an image must contain a research "tangible"—often specific to a discipline. For disaster researchers, such tangibles might be social interaction, social relationships, processes, and inter-organizational coordination.

For example, a photographic sequence might capture the reconstruction of a home and the volunteer crews that rebuild the unit. By capturing images from debris removal through house dedications, the steps and stages in the reconstruction process are revealed. In addition, photos can capture the inter-organizational partnerships necessary to rebuild a community or the development of relationships between volunteer crews and homeowners. Imagine also, the photos that might be generated by researchers, organizational representatives, volunteer crews, and homeowners—by putting cameras into their hands, a diverse set of perspectives can be generated producing a richer insight into the disaster recovery process.

Visual Data Techniques

Traditional techniques associated with visual methods include using photographs and videos through four main methods: *native photography, photo-elicitation, photo documentation,* and *photo-therapeutic intervention.* Each of these offers relevance for disaster studies. The first technique, *native photography,* places image-capturing tools into the hands of insiders to gain their emic perspective. Directions may vary from "capture your day" to concentrating on a theme such as "the arrival of unannounced volunteers." Also called auto-photography or subject-generated photography, native insider (emic) use allows us to look through the eyes of those directly involved for what they see (Collier and Collier 1986; Worth and Adair 1972). Analysis of native photographs can occur through the use of an expert panel that analyzes the imagery or through content analysis.

What typically enriches visual analysis is the second technique, *photo-elicitation* (Harper 2002), where the researcher interviews the subject about the images taken by the subject. This combination of techniques was used after Hurricane Katrina when shelter residents took photographs and were then interviewed about the content (Pike, Reeves, Phillips 2006). Through the interviews, several themes emerged that showed the pain endured by survivors as they built meaningful relationships in temporary locations. Survivors found dinner tables to be particularly important locations where they processed their experiences and built meaningful relationships. Researchers may also ask the interviewee to write about the images as a means of self-reflection. In short, photo-elicitation involves the researcher and subject in mutually discerning the meaning of the images (Blinn and Harrist 1991; Rose 2007). Does it work? A study that looked at the technique with control and experimental groups found that the pictures produced longer interviews that were "more comprehensive" and also helped "subjects overcome the fatigue and repetition of conventional interviews." Control interviews were "less structured, rambling, and freer in association" that produced data considered "precise and, at times, even encyclopedic" (Harper 2002, p. 14). Film elicitation, used far less than photographs, may be overwhelming to analyze or use. However, it would be interesting to use such films—perhaps old civil defense films vis-à-vis more recent homeland security videos—to reveal the ways in which countries and agencies have explained threats and prepared the public. Social media tools, such as YouTube, remain un-analyzed for their potential impact. In the United States, the www.youtube.com/ FEMA site represents a rich depository of visual images waiting for analysis.

A third technique, *photo-documentation*, asks the researcher to capture data on a particular theme such as inter-organizational coordination, the establishment of an incident command location, or the ways in which a recovery effort expands in a fixed site. Within the photo/video-documentation, the technique of saturation directs the researcher to take images of everything deemed relevant to the theme. Enormous amounts of visual data may result, which provides depth but generates a staggering amount of analytical work. Other sampling techniques may direct the researcher to capture images more systematically. For example, to capture the reconstruction process, the researcher may want to return at specific times (perhaps monthly intervals) and photograph the nth house on the block every time. In disaster research, this "time and place sampling" is particularly useful. By capturing an image temporally and spatially, a researcher can place the reconstruction into time sequence—which would likely yield differential rates of recovery for various groups. With an overlay by spatial location, patterns of historic segregation, income disparity, and age of household might be discernible (Cutter 2006).

Disaster scholars may want to consider the perspective of the visual image. For example, a photograph of a toy fire truck placed on a destroyed vehicle yields information into the loss sustained by a child and suggestive of the loss of innocence and safety. A more macro-level image also produces useful content. Taken further away, the fire truck toy fades into a broader context. Taken in the Lower Ninth Ward after Hurricane Katrina, such an image reveals losses of social relationships across a neighborhood destroyed and devoid of social interaction. From an even broader view, satellite images reveal the neighborhood in an even broader context—the city of New Orleans—where 80% of the entire urban area went under water and caused an evacuation of nearly half a million people.

A final technique, *phototherapeutic intervention*, has not been used in disaster studies. The technique, though, offers a useful tool, especially for psychological research in disasters. Large-scale or traumatic events typically are captured in some way by the public or security cameras. Such images can be used in therapy sessions, support groups, and in research. Images taken during a disaster are often used during debriefings and "hot washes" (when emergency managers discuss what went right and wrong and revise their plans for the next event). Visual images, coupled with interviewing, can enable those affected to discuss and process their experience. Such an approach would fit well with focus groups, critical incident stress debriefings, and psychological therapy.

Summary

This chapter has provided an overview of issues associated with QDR along with techniques for data collection. Though the techniques remain the same across all social sciences, it is the context of conducting qualitative disaster research that must be considered. Despite the challenges associated with disaster studies, a rich body of knowledge has been generated that informs theory, practice, and policy. In the next chapter, we turn to data analysis procedures, some of which are indeed unique to disaster studies.

3

WRITING-UP THE METHODS SECTION

Overview of the Chapter

Multiple techniques exist to analyze and write up qualitative data, with none unique to disaster studies. Indeed, qualitative disaster analysis relies on standard techniques with rigorous approaches common to other social sciences. This chapter introduces readers to the process of analyzing and writing up qualitative disaster research. To do so, the chapter includes three main parts: processing and managing data, analyzing data, and writing up a methods section. A detailed example of how to write up a methods section concludes the chapter.

Processing and Managing Data

Many qualitative researchers become overwhelmed with the sheer amount of data that can accumulate, even in a short time. Thus, a necessary first step is to organize and "process" the data. Doing so begins with the first moment of data collection, by ensuring that necessary paperwork and IRB procedures are followed. Either hard copy or electronic files should be organized, with notes, transcripts, and other materials from each interviewee placed into a de-identified file. To insure confidentiality, most IRBs will require that names not be included in such a file. Numbering related materials, and keeping a numbered list with names in a separate location, is usually what most IRBs would expect.

As time passes, files will continue to accumulate. Remembering what document is in which file can be difficult. To manage such material, some researchers create databases (see Table 3.1). Each database will differ, but some elements may be consistent. For social scientists, demographic information may be crucial. For qualitative disaster researchers, disaster-specific information may be needed. Entry fields in a database might then include:

- *Demographics.* Gender, age, race/ethnicity, age, disability, household size (before and after), languages in the home, time since immigration, income, education, etc.
- *Information critical to the research question.* Time spent in a shelter, number of moves made before reaching permanent shelter.
- *The disaster.* Location, type, magnitude, scope.
- *Impacts.* Dollar losses, property losses, injuries, deaths, overall damage to the broader neighborhood or community.
- *Conditions pertinent to the study.* Insurance coverage, rental availability, economics of the area.

Spreadsheet databases can be used, but researchers may also want to compile a database for import into statistical packages as well.

Table 3.1
Sample Database

Case Number	Gender	Age	Disaster	Location	Number of Deaths in Family	Days Spent in Temporary Shelter	Number of Moves until Reaching Permanent Shelter
1	F	6	Tsunami	Sri Lanka	3	42	8
2	M	42	Tsunami	India	7	17	4
3	F	33	Tsunami	Thailand	2	13	2

Yes, it is acceptable to include quantitative data in a qualitative study, and the database can serve as an important set of variables for subsequent analysis.

Quantitative statistical analysis is not the only way that computers can be used to examine qualitative data. A number of qualitative software packages exist that can serve multiple purposes:

- To organize data into a comprehensive and connected set of electronic files
- To begin the data reduction process
- To expedite the data reduction process
- To allow researchers to more easily review and reassign codes through linked files
- To incorporate data beyond transcription, including visual data, documents, and observational notes (depending on the software package)
- To generate reports that organize the coded content into separate files linked back to the original source
- To manage categories of information and uncover connections and meanings between them
- To assist the researcher in creating analytical products such as taxonomies

Qualitative software package do not replace researchers. You must do the analytical work, with assistance from a program that can efficiently code transcription data and move it into an appropriately assigned category (Richards 2009; 1999). At present, it appears that the majority of qualitative disaster researchers do not use qualitative software programs, although that appears to be changing.

Mitchell et al. (2004) used QSR NVivo to reveal that volunteers managing a jetliner crash failed to seek mental health support. Subsequently, higher levels of personal trauma were reported, suggesting that volunteers would have benefited from pre-event training and post-event counseling. MacDonal and colleagues (2012) reported on a longitudinal study of emotional reactions to Australian bushfires. They also used QSR NVivo to identify themes embedded within their twenty-five interviews. This study relied on the coding and model-building features of the software program to identify a range of life events (including the bushfire) and the need for communities to realize that disasters are only one of many life events that influence emotional responses in a five-to-six-year post-disaster period. Eisenman et al. (2009) used ATLAS.ti to examine focus group data on low income Latinos. They uncovered themes revealing that disaster preparedness programs must be culturally appropriate. Latinos in their study wanted help with developing family community plans and details about quantities of materials in ready kits.

Software thus functions as a means to organize, code, link, and analyze data efficiently. Output can be used to demonstrate to journal reviewers, committee members, and colleagues that you have coded the data consistently and accurately. Software packages like QSR NVivo (which offers a thirty day free trial), ATLAS.ti, Qualitative Data Analysis Program (QDAP, which is open source), and others can facilitate data reduction and analysis, provide written and visual records of coded material and analytical tools, and make coded categories readily available for writing up findings. But it all starts with data analysis techniques, which we turn to next.

Data Analysis

Despite variation across social science data analysis techniques, the majority of data analysis techniques have several elements in common. First, data analysis involves researchers in first reducing massive amounts of data to glean core insights. Imagine, for example, the daunting task faced by Chetkovich (1997), who studied the lived experiences of women and minorities as they entered the traditionally white and male fire service. With over four thousand pages of interview transcripts, she needed to hone in on the key findings and write up the study for various audiences. Data analysis techniques thus enable researchers to reduce data and identify core findings.

A second common element is the timing of data analysis. Most qualitative researchers begin analysis at the beginning of the study. For example, a researcher would transcribe initial interviews or write up detailed observational notes. Taking a step back from the data-gathering process, the researcher would turn to a recording of the interview or read through the transcript or observational notes—usually several times. Lofland et al. (2006) describe this process well. At the start of a project, the researcher spends the majority of time gathering data, while simultaneously analyzing the information. As the study moves on, the data gathering decreases as the data analysis increases. Early analysis guides the researcher to discern emergent properties of the data, uncover unexpected findings, and refine the study. Spradley (1980) uses his twelve-step "Developmental Research Sequence" similarly, to move the researcher toward deeper, richer, and more nuanced insights, generating increasingly focused understanding of the social setting and its cultural elements.

Third, researchers spend a lot of time with their data. It is valuable to review transcripts, visual and documentary data, and observational notes regularly. Good researchers read and re-read their data, becoming intimately familiar with the diverse and subjective realities that people share through their words, actions, documents, and images. Researchers often talk about "listening" until the data "speak" to them. No, they are not crazy; rather, they are waiting for consistent meanings to emanate from the data. To do so, read through your transcripts and listen to the recordings of your interviews. You will hear words commonly repeated and themes will emerge. Quite frequently, people will use the same phrase. After hurricane Katrina in the U.S., for example, people often said "this one is different" in referring to the scope and magnitude of the event—and also of the challenges faced by response and recovery organizations (Phillips 2013). Seasoned researchers, and students well-versed in the research literature, will experience this phenomenon. Knowing what the literature has already found will enable you to "hear" these findings and guide you to a more rigorous analysis that confirms or negates what the data "speak" to you.

A fourth common element is to "code," or categorize, the data using various techniques. Coding is a data reduction process that focuses inquiry and enables researchers to assess what they are hearing, determine if the instrument needs to be tweaked, decide if the sample is producing robust information, and choose when to end the study. We turn to the coding process next.

Coding

Coding is the process of applying a shortened name or phrase to a portion of data within transcripts, notes, documents, or even visual images. To illustrate, consider what type of code or shortened name you might apply to these quotes from my study on faith-based organizations:

> One evening a week they invited people to their camp which was a wonderful way to build relationships. It was like "one big happy family."
>
> It is just their way of walking in, like they have always been in your community. They did not judge or question locals. It was like they walked in and they were family.
>
> It was like they were family. They invited me out to eat dinner, participate in the singing, the food was good.
>
> They also came to our events like Carnival, they enjoyed themselves! It was like one big family. They have big hearts.

If you picked "Like Family," then you chose the same code that I did. Now, imagine that you have to read through 160 such transcripts (x 25 pages each = 4,000 pages total). After doing so, you will have amassed a file of similar quotes pulled from those data. You now feel confident regarding the code, representing a theme that clearly emerged from the data, and the leading way that homeowners describe volunteers.

Coding can occur in several ways. Semi- or openly-structured approaches to coding data characterize most qualitative research and QDR is no different. Semi or open coding usually relies on general, initial codes that emerge from the data—as the example on "like family" illustrates. A researcher doing this open kind of coding might work through the data, jotting down ideas for codes, and then refining the codes by re-reading the data and comparing one transcript or set of notes to another. A similar but more structured initial approach is to start with major categories from the interview guide. For example, a study on warnings might have initial codes of "first heard," or "initial response," or "degree of belief." As the researcher reads through the transcripts, they can modify those codes to more closely fit the data. But there is more to coding. Now that you have coded content into this theme, you can delve further to discern deeper and richer meanings about the relationships between homeowners and volunteers. Next, we turn to some specific techniques that move researchers through additional, deeper coding procedures.

Domain, Taxonomic, and Componential Analysis (Spradley 1980)

Anthropologist James P. Spradley (1980) approached the data analysis process by creating a twelve-step "Developmental Research Sequence (DRS)." He wanted to lead analysts from making initial observations into developing increasingly focused understanding of cultural elements embedded within social settings. The first four steps in the DRS direct researchers to locate a social situation, conduct data gathering (e.g., interviews or observations), make an "ethnographic record" (take notes, record interviews), and then make descriptive observations (fully flesh out the details of the observations, and interviews). Step 5 is called "domain analysis" and guides the researcher to begin identifying what they see and hear in the data. Fortunately, Spradley provides a set of ways to think about the data, as few things are worse than staring at a blinking cursor wondering where to start.

Spradley tells us that we should start looking for a "cover term" that represents a *cultural domain*, such as firefighters, emergency managers, survivors, or volunteers. He then says to search the data for examples of included terms that fall under the main cover term. To do so, he provides nine "semantic relationships" (Spradley 1980, see below). Probably the easiest semantic relationship to start with is called "strict inclusion," which he graphs visually as "x is a kind of y." The x represents an "included term," with the y serving as the cover term. Domain analysis allows researchers to dig into the data, searching for information that helps to organize the data. Imagine, for example, that you have read through multiple transcripts representing several hundreds of pages to identify the organizational structure of a Fire Department. The domain analysis allows you to take a first cut at the kinds of personnel found within the department. To illustrate, think about the *cover* (y) term of firefighters, which might *include* (x) career firefighters, volunteer firefighters, rookie, or officer firefighters. Graphically, such a domain analysis would look like Table 3.2.

Table 3.2 **Domain Analysis**	
Y **Cover Term**	**Kinds of Firefighters** (**Strict inclusion, x *is a kind of* y**)
x	Career
x	Volunteer
x	Rookie
x	Officer

Other kinds of semantic relationships to generate domain analyses include:

- *Spatial* (*x* is a place in *y*, such as the EOC is a place in the emergency management agency);
- *Cause-effect* (*x* is a result of *y*, or wildfire is a result of D4 Severe Drought Level Conditions);
- *Rationale* (*x* is a reason for doing *y*, or learning organizational roles is a reason for conducting exercises);
- *Location-for-action* (*x* is a place for doing *y*, or the local community center is a place for establishing disaster recovery centers);
- *Function* (*x* is used for *y*, or Long-Term Recovery Committees are used to organize local, grass-roots reconstruction efforts);
- *Means-end* (*x* is a way to do *y*, or convening public charettes is a way to involve stakeholders in recovery planning);
- *Sequence* (*x* is a step in doing *y*, or moving into temporary housing is a step in returning to permanent housing);
- *Attribution* (*x* is a characteristic of *y*, or good communication skills are characteristic of FEMA Voluntary Agency Liaisons).

For Spradley, domain analysis guides the researcher to focus on a rich area for continued study. Ideally, early domain analysis focuses the researcher and enables the study to become richer and deeper. Domain analysis should also send us back to the field for more focused investigations (Step 6). Spradley continues moving us to higher-level understanding of cultural elements in social

Table 3.3
Taxonomic Analysis
Types of Firefighters/FF (Strict Inclusion)

1. Types of firefighters on staff
  a. Paid
    i. Career FF
      1. Structural (Full-Time)
      2. Wildland (Seasonal)
  b. Not Paid
    i. Volunteer FF
2. Types of structural firefighter ranks
  a. Firefighters
    i. Trainee/Recruit/Probationary Firefighter
    ii. Firefighter I
    iii. Firefighter II
    iv. Firefighter III
    v. Driver Operator/Engineer
  b. Fire Officers
    i. Lieutenant
    ii. Captain
    iii. Battalion Chief
    iv. Deputy Chief/Assistant Chief
    v. Division Chief
    vi. Chief

Source: with appreciation to Barbara Russo, Fayetteville State University, North Carolina.

settings by asking researchers to select domains for more intensive investigation. Step 7 involves analysts in constructing a taxonomy, which is not unlike an outline that shows sets and sub-sets of inter-related information. To illustrate, let's look at one of the domains mentioned previously, using an outline format to present the data (for other options, see Spradley 1980, see Table 3.3).

Spradley follows the taxonomic analysis by recommending that the researcher increase their observations selectively (Step 8). Again, the researcher returns to the field, zeroing in on the research question to understand more and to produce richer insights. Analytically, Step 9 directs the analyst to create a componential analysis, in which you look for attributes of the various

Table 3.4
Componential Analysis

Domain	Years in rank and file	Gender	Family history in firefighting
Trainee	<1	4% female; 96% male	Somewhat common
Captains	7–10	3% female; 97% male	Quite common
Majors	>15	2% female; 98% male	Very common
Deputy Chiefs	>20	1% female; 99% male	Very common
Chiefs	>25	.5% female; 99.5% male	Nearly all

Source: with appreciation to Barbara Russo, Fayetteville State University, North Carolina.

categories previously unveiled. The componential analysis promotes contrasts across the categories. Following on the taxonomy above, a preliminary componential analysis and might initially look like Table 3.4.

The purpose of the componential analysis is to reveal variation and similarities. In Table 3.4, we can see that becoming a firefighter and moving up into the higher ranks of officers is more common among men who come from families with an occupational legacy of firefighting. Spradley urges researcher to complete the developmental research sequence by using these analyses to discover cultural themes ("Firefighting is a Gender-Specific, Familial-Based Occupation," Step 10); taking a cultural inventory (Step 11, are there gaps in your information?); and writing an ethnography of the results (Step 12, for a relevant example, see Chetkovich 1997).

The "C" Model (Quarantelli 1987b)

Students and graduates of the Disaster Research Center know the "C" Model quite well, the only data reduction effort to specifically address disasters (Quarantelli 1987b; Quarantelli 2002). Essentially, the C Model represents a way to look at elements of one's data as a means to develop a case study. Quarantelli explains "in scientific research we are usually trying to make some statements about one or more of four possible aspects, all of which start with the letter C" (Quarantelli 1987b, p. 7).

The "C" stands for words that begin with the letter C and have varied over time: Chronology/Career, Characteristics, Conditions, and Consequences are the most common. Essentially, the C Model is a way to unpack and then re-organize one's data. As Quarantelli (1987b, p. 7) explains "conditions or circumstances which lead to certain characteristics which will have consequences as a result of the career of the phenomena." The key is to know what falls into each element of the C Model so that one selects the correct information for each element.

- *Conditions.* Conditions "generate a particular phenomenon that shows certain characteristics." Deductive theorists may want to think of conditions as the critical independent variables. Inductive theorists identify conditions specific to a setting that may influence matters. For example, an experienced FEMA Voluntary Agency Liaison (VAL) or faith-based organization may be instrumental in fostering development and sustainability of a local Long-Term Recovery Committee (LTRC). Or, delays in providing government funding to an area affected by from a superstorm means that people stay longer in shelters and recovery languishes. Uncovering conditions can be challenging and, though Quarantelli lists this element as first, it may be easier to do the chronology or career first. Lofland (et al. 2006) call this the "trace-back" method—an event unfolds (e.g., the power grid goes down during a geomagnetic storm). What other conditions worsened or precipitated that event (e.g., aging infrastructure, tightly coupled systems)?
- *Characteristics.* Quarantelli (1987b, p. 7) indicates that characteristics can clearly be "informed by empirical observations." In practice, most researchers that focus on characteristics using the C-Model do so by peeling away the structure or essential elements of a given phenomenon under study. For example, the composition of a search and rescue group might be formal or

informal, or both (Lois 2003). Similarly, LTRCs might be characterized as hierarchical, collaborative, or even completely unorganized. People in shelters typically come from lower-income households; a longitudinal study of a shelter would probably identify characteristics of those most likely to linger (e.g., disability, see NOD 2005) due to various conditions (e.g, lack of accessible government housing, see *FEMA v. Brou* 2005).

- *Consequences.* The outcomes are called consequences, which can be manifest (intended), latent (unintended), positive, or negative. To illustrate, think about these possibilities:
  - *Manifest.* Repairs began on damaged homes and new homes began to be built as a result of the organizational structure of the LTRC, available funds, and incoming volunteers.
  - *Latent.* Strong relationships developed between homeowners and volunteers, generating a sense of hope and normalcy that provided psychological comfort and spiritual sustenance.
  - *Positive.* People returned to their homes and jobs, enabling the community to begin to rebound economically.
  - *Negative.* Harsh feelings developed between those selected for volunteer assistance by the local Long Term Recovery Committee and those who did not receive assistance.
- *Chronology/Career.* Good qualitative research tells a story, representing the lived experience of those who went through an event. The initial section of a C Model case study walks a reader through what happened, when it happened, and how it happened. Much of the time, just asking people to "tell me when you realized the hurricane was coming" launches their story. By reading across transcripts, a researcher can glean the common steps experienced by those who faced the storm: hearing the warning, confirming the warning, deciding where and how to evacuate, finding a shelter, waiting until the storm passed, looking at satellite images of flooded neighborhoods, applying for recovery assistance, and moving into temporary housing. Another approach might be to describe the career of a Long-Term Recovery Committee (LTRC): the FEMA Voluntary Agency Liaison (VAL) convened a meeting, concerned community

members showed up, a temporary organization developed, leaders emerged, a non-profit organization emerged and became legal, funds came into the organization, case managers brought needed repair cases to the LTRC, faith-based organizations offered volunteers, and homeowners met people who "became like family."

Empirical research uncovers the "C" model elements, which are ultimately written up and presented in sequential order: "Conditions (C1)→Characteristics (C2)→Consequences (C3)→Careers (C4)" (Quarantelli 1987, p. 7). The C Model is not unlike Strauss and Corbin (1993):

Causal conditions→Phenomenon→Context→Intervening conditions→Action/interaction→Consequences.

Regardless, case studies using structured elements represent the most likely format for presenting findings (Strauss and Corbin 1993). Ultimately, writing up the C elements depends on choices one makes on how to present the story (see Chapter 4).

Grounded Theory (Glaser and Strauss 1967)

Undoubtedly, the most commonly used approach within QDR is grounded theory. Glaser and Strauss (1967) created a systematic approach to generating theory from qualitative data, though ultimately each author went separate directions (Glaser 1992; Strauss and Corbin 1993). Originally, grounded theory developed when other researchers wanted to understand how Glaser and Strauss gleaned meaningful, theoretically rich insights into the how medical staff managed emotional work around dying patients (Glaser and Strauss 1965). Both emphasized that being in the field helped to capture theoretical insights. Theoretical explanations then emanated from systematic efforts *grounded* in coding the data. They illustrated concepts with the data, which they captured effectively by presenting narratives that walked readers into the lived experience of those under study.

Grounded theory begins by analyzing data as they are gathered, and by comparing bits of information systematically to discern similarities and differences. Through constantly comparing the coded data, the researcher insures that they have coded consistently. The coding process then proceeds to move the researcher from general insights to increasingly specific foci, honing in on and understanding the core concept embedded in people's stories. Doing so requires the analyst to read, read, and then read again the interview transcripts, observation notes, or research documents. The ultimate goals include "parsimony and scope," two essential elements of good scientific work. *Parsimony* means that you can encapsulate content efficiently, perhaps within a single concept, such as "interoperability." For first responders and emergency managers, *interoperability* refers to the ability to communicate with and across each other's organizational units. The problem is that, historically, different departments and offices have purchased various kinds of equipment that does not always "talk" to each other. Imagine the challenges after a major terrorist attack, when police and fire cannot communicate with each other directly. *Scope* means that you can account for a wider amount of data, such as the various kinds of interoperability, such as technological (communications equipment variances across first responder units) and cultural (inter-organizational ways of working and connecting). As an example, think about the widespread use of the language and framework of the Incident Command System (ICS). However, many non-governmental organizations have lagged in adopting ICS, which impairs abilities to understand how a response might be organized, where resources come from, who is in charge—and much more (Neal and Webb 2006). The concept of "interoperability" captures a range of challenges associated with effective inter-organizational response, insuring both parsimony and scope. So, how does a grounded theorist get to that powerful, single concept?

Glaser and Strauss (1967) relied on "open coding" as the first cut at deciphering data. Open coding begins as you read through the data, examining and comparing the information. When content seems similar (e.g., "interoperability issues"), you code it as such. When the next similar content appears on "interoperability issues," you compare that content to the previous content. This procedure is called the "constant comparative method." To illustrate further, flip back to the quotes on how homeowners felt about volunteers, where the code "like family" seemed to fit. Now, compare carefully the words in each of the separate quotes. Are you sure they fit the category of "like family"? Next, look for similarities and dissimilarities in the data. Are there instances where homeowners referred to the volunteers differently? Were other words used? Or, did you find subjective differences within the term "like family"? Those differences might reveal important nuances, such as: "family who call to check on us," or "family who come to visit." This deeper analysis sheds light on how people define family as well as their expectations for continued relationships after the volunteerism ends.

The constant comparative method allows you to verify your initial observations, develop your theoretical explanation, and be more accurate with coding (Glaser and Strauss 1967). Table 3.5 presents an opportunity to conduct such an open-coding effort (for the results, see Phillips, Garza and Neal 1994).

Categories (e.g., interoperability, family) then need to be further examined to uncover their properties. A category stands by itself as a main element encapsulating significant and meaningful portions of the data. Properties represent an element of the category (Glaser and Strauss 1967). Think about emergency managers discussing their EOC. Is it a traditional, fixed site (Neal 2003, 2005)? Or, perhaps it is a mobile site that relies on large vehicles to provide support? Maybe the EOC has been set up temporarily in a tent because the tornado destroyed the main EOC (as happened in Birmingham, Alabama in 2011)? Maybe the emergency manager is discussing a virtual EOC? Properties of the categories can then be examined further to reveal dimensions of the properties: What is the size of each EOC? What kinds of communications features does each contain? How many people can work inside the unit (an interesting question for the virtual EOC!)? What is the noise level? Does bandwidth influence EOC capabilities? Revealing properties and dimensions is the task of selective coding, where you focus in on the core category as a means to provide the richness and depth so desired in QDR.

Sjoberg, Wallenius and Larsson (2006) used grounded theory to look at leadership in complex rescue operations. They started by transcribing the interviews and then relying on the constant comparative methods developed by Glaser and Strauss. They initially did open coding, and then the "codes were sorted into different categories" (p. 578). An example of a primary category became

Table 3.5

Try Your Hand at Open Coding (Phillips, Garza and Neal 1994)

- You can't ignore misinformation. . . it's like playing fire chief. We've got a 600,000 acre fire and a 4 inch garden hose.
- Outsiders like me from California, if you don't know the area, you're dead because there are no signs anymore. What really happens is you get close and hope you'll find someone who knows better than you.
- The majority of the people here are Spanish speakers. We have translators walking around, delivering messages to all the homes. . . the information where all the distribution centers are, the American Red Cross.
- There are undocumented aliens who are terrified that if they are found out they'll be sent home. . . if anything even looking like a military or law enforcement agent. . . they flee. . .
- Everybody has been real cooperative, it is just the magnitude is so huge. You will hear a lot of criticisms of every agency but I do not know if that is fair criticism.
- We had portable radios right after it happened but they never really worked. The army now has radios and they have been real cooperative about getting word around, but at first, before they really got here, that was really difficult for us.

"everyday working conditions." This category evolved into favorable and unfavorable working conditions. Ultimately, four additional codes emerged as influential on individual and organizational leadership: training and exercises (favorable in providing experience); previous mission experiences (unfavorable when they did not provide relevant experience); personal knowledge of co-actors (favorable from knowing each other); and organizational climate (unfavorable when conflict existed, p. 580). Sjoberg and colleagues then proceeded to the final step in grounded theory, to demonstrate the linkages between the categories (which Spradley refers to as a taxonomy). They did so by thinking through the categories:

Organization of the rescue operation (before, during, after); Experiences and competences (individually, group, and organization); Factors in the environment (other organizations, media, the public); Stress reactions (individually, group, organization); Leadership and decision making (general description, problems, dilemmas, etc.); Outcome (of the whole operation, both positive and negative); verbatim, p. 578).

The researchers then developed a model which identified key conditions that should enhance leadership in future rescue operations.

Using a More Structured Approach to Coding (Bogdan and Biklen 1992)

Students approaching coding for the first time may find an open or unstructured approach, like those described here, somewhat challenging. Sometimes, you find yourself frustrated, staring at the blinking cursor waiting for the data to "speak" to you. As a useful exercise, it might prove worthwhile to use a more structured approach. One such effort comes from the educational researchers Bogdan and Biklen (1992), who direct data analysts to make decisions that narrow the study. They provide a set of initial ways to look at and listen to the data. As you read through the data, look for certain kinds of phenomena to appear, and insert additional ideas for codes in the margins (a word processor is useful for this initial effort, though computer software programs can be used and then edited as needed). Examples of useful questions follow, using the post-disaster recovery planning period as the setting:

- *Setting-context codes.* Where is the location of the planning event? Is it by the side of a damaged bayou community? In a community center? Is it a formal workshop led by a consultant? Perhaps it is a charette inviting people to comment as they walk past ideas posted in a public mall?
- *Definition of the situation codes.* How do participants and planners define the situation? Thomas and Thomas (1928) said "if you define a situation as real, it is real in its consequences." Is the planning event an opportunity to transform the community into a more resilient locale able to rebound from another strike? Or, is this an opportunity to use land-use planning and other government

techniques to take land and displace people, as some
locals have felt after hurricane Katrina and other events?

- *Subjects' ways of thinking about people and objects.*
Do the invited participants think of each other as
trustworthy and credible? Do they see the consultant
as knowledgeable about local culture and ways of life?
How do locals perceive historic properties and cultural
resources, what do they think and feel about the potential
loss of meaningful places?

- *Process codes.* How has the planning event been designed?
Are there stages and steps for the people and community
to walk through? Are there methods by which people
can share ideas through verbal, written, or online means?
How are decisions to be made regarding options for
rebuilding the community?

- *Activity codes.* What are people doing behind the scenes
of the planning event to set it up? What happens once
the event starts? How formally structured is the event?
Do people sit and debate, or mill about and chat? Is there
food? Child care?

- *Event codes.* When and where is the planning event?
Is it held at a formal location? Who comes or does
not come?

- *Strategy codes.* How do planners announce the event?
What efforts are made to engage the public? What do
they try to do to pull people's ideas out of all kind of
participants, from verbose to extremely shy?

- *Relationship and social structure codes.* How do people
seem to inter-relate? Are elected officials perceived the
same as everyday citizens? How do they connect, talk, and
communicate (verbally and non-verbally). How effective
is the relationship between the citizens, elected officials,
planners, consultants, insiders, and outsiders?

- *Methods codes.* What questions emerge? Are the
methodological techniques sufficient to capture the
unfolding story or phenomena? Is the sample relevant
and sufficient? Is the process moving from initial ideas to
richer and deeper insights on an increasingly selective and
focused topic? What answers to the research questions are
beginning to emerge?

- *Preassigned coding systems.* Funders, dissertation committees, and others who bear some kind of influence on the research may direct the researcher to identify specific kinds of codes. One might start with an interview instrument, breaking down the questions on the instrument as initial coding categories: warnings, evacuation, sheltering, temporary housing, rebuilding efforts.

Writing a Memo

From the point of inception, all researchers should generate memos. Doing so becomes the first step toward writing up the coded information into a final paper, thesis, dissertation, publication, or book. Most QR, and thus QDR, begins with writing a memo, which can vary in type, length, and content. A memo written early in the research project usually captures initial impressions. It can be as simple as Box 3.1.

Spradley (1980) provides good ideas for writing up a memo in his notions of the mini- and grand tour. The mini-tour focuses in on a concentrated area, such as the effort among volunteers to install a door during reconstruction including a description of the

---

Box 3.1 **MEMO: Impressions of Katrina Debris**

August 30, 2005, Pass Christian, Mississippi.

Followed the National Guard as units removed road debris while en route to the coast. Upon arrival in Pass Christian, located more impassable roads. Multiple kinds of debris can be discerned while walking through affected areas: porches torn from houses, hazardous chemicals strewn through neighborhoods, clothing and furniture thoroughly soaked and mildewing fast, and slowly increasing areas where MRE cartons and empty water bottles are beginning to accumulate. Survivors can be seen searching for personal items, a process made difficult because storm surge moved houses from their foundations and down the street. Experiencing concern for exposure to contaminated areas for survivors and research team.

door and tools as well as the division of labor, supervision of the volunteers, and homeowner reaction. A grand-tour memo would provide a broader brush image of the volunteer site, describing the multiple locations within a home where volunteers paint, repair, install, and do other rebuilding activities. Others try aggregate-type approaches, such as attempting to describe kinds of homeless persons (Snow and Anderson 1993) or a typical day (see Box 3.2).

Box 3.2 A Week in the Life of Katrina Volunteers (by Brenda Phillips)

Loaded vans roll into camp late Sunday afternoon after long days on the road from Pennsylvania, Oregon, Iowa, and farther north... Manitoba, Winnipeg, and Saskatchewan. Stiff volunteers emerge, stretch their limbs, and pull out duffels and sleeping bags. They look around, slowly taking in the water marks—well over their heads—on nearby buildings. Huge barges move slowly down the Mississippi River. The energetic, smiling long-term crew spills out of RVs to greet them warmly, then guide all into dormitory-like rooms. Inside, they see hand-made bunk beds stickered with the name tags of previous occupants.

The project director welcomes everyone for orientation, then leads them in prayer. Everyone fills out volunteer forms indicating skill levels and backgrounds. Expertise varies from "none" to "can supervise others." The project director addresses safety first, from using harnesses while working on elevated sites to goggles for painters and careful footwork to avoid painful fire ant bites. Sage advice, "Leave your ego here," guides the volunteers as they begin to think about the tasks ahead. A home on the bayou needs a new boat dock so that a returning family can earn a livelihood again. Another needs plumbing and electrical work so that the resident, displaced the past five years now, can finally return home. An office manager tells the volunteers to drink lots of fluids as the heat and humidity will be stifling.

Sunday night is the cook's night off, so new arrivals head out for dinner. By 6:30, most have returned. Some sit around the table talking quietly. Others play ping pong or pool, work on puzzles, enjoy board games, watch television, or jump on Facebook using the wireless connection. Quite a few watch television—sports like

World Cup soccer or the World Series, or secondary choices like nature shows. Soft guitar music rises out of the men's dorm and voices join together on a favorite tune. Heads turn as the project director walks back in to write on the white board: Volunteers move forward to learn whose home they will work on. Those tasked with elevation work shift aside to look at diagrams explaining how poles are placed, braced, and squared. Nearby, cooks set out big coolers and beverage canisters for early morning use. The office manager sweeps in, cell phone clipped to her belt, and asks everyone to double-check their contact information taken from volunteer forms, and already entered into the Mennonite Disaster Service (MDS) database. By 10 p.m. lights go out and everyone tries to fall asleep, still excited about the week ahead.

6 a.m., Monday morning. If you are not already up, you can hear others stirring, and it's time to rise. No shower this morning, just throw on work clothes and head to the dining room to prepare a sack lunch. Walking in, you see long-term volunteers refilling coffee cups and conferring. The office manager checks in every few minutes with the project director and construction supervisor, then writes today's heat index on the board: 108 degrees Fahrenheit. Earlier risers have begun working their way along a table laden with meats, cheeses, condiments, chips, cookies, vegetables, and fruit. Figuring out the system, each volunteer picks up a name tag, drops their lunch into the numbered cooler for the assigned project site, and sits down to await breakfast. Delicious smells fill the dining room as cooks bustle in and out of the kitchen placing large containers of pancakes, sausages, and eggs alongside cereal, oatmeal, and toast made from homemade bread. As the cook calls "ready," the project director asks everyone to pray, then selects who gets to go first: sometimes by table, other times by age or geographic location. At 7:25, a volunteer leads morning devotions by reading a chosen scripture and reflecting on its meaning for the work ahead. At 7:30, the project director reviews the day's assignments, then crew leaders take volunteers out to select tools, paint brushes, ladders, power cords, and other materials needed on the site. Some volunteers lack familiarity, so long-termers stand ready to assist and ensure they get the right tools for the job. Short-termers liberally apply sunscreen and for those working in bayous, a good dousing of insect repellant as well. Everyone piles into the correct van with the numbered coolers and heads to the project site by 8 a.m.

Driving through the damaged area brings meaning to the work. Stunned, volunteers see sofas shoved against windows, kitchen appliances pushed into living rooms, and mold everywhere: on *everything*. No one is home in this neighborhood. Vans loaded with volunteers move into the project site where bulldozers have removed people's homes, leaving weedy, overgrown lots now infested with rodents. One home stands alone on a single block, with FEMA trailers scattered along the rest of the neighborhood.

One van stops at a house under construction, elevated 10 feet into the air and framed by last week's crew. As they exit the van, the front door of a trailer opens and an elderly woman steps down gingerly with her cane. Smiling broadly, she extends her hand in welcome and drawls in an unfamiliar Cajun accent, "My angels are here!"

Another Mennonite Disaster Service truck pulls up with supplies, lumber, shingles, sheetrock, long-handled roller brushes, large containers of paint, whatever the crew needs. Teamwork emerges as the central skill truly needed, with crew leaders guiding volunteers to work assignments. Communication supports effective team work, and crew leaders and more experienced volunteers answer questions and offer advice to improve efforts. As the work comes along, some crews sing favorite hymns while others josh mildly about skill levels. There is a fifteen-minute break around 10, and at noon, everyone sits down for lunch. In the city, heat and humidity settles oppressively, abated somewhat by over-sized fans blowing air through the home. On a bayou site, a breeze stirs the waters and cools everyone a bit. The sights and sounds of an unfamiliar environment make lunch even more intriguing— an otter frolics near a dock, dolphins web and flow through murky waters, pelicans glide overhead, and wary volunteers keep an eye out for fire ants, snakes, and the occasional alligator. Thirty minutes later it's time to work again, with frequent breaks to re-apply sunscreen, hydrate, and remind each other of safety precautions. At mid-afternoon the project director appears. He does not dally, moving with purpose to converse briefly with the construction supervisor, then reappears an hour later with needed supplies. By 4, it's time to clean up the work site, load the vans, and head back to camp.

Sweaty, tired, and muddy, short-termers return to clean up. A refreshing shower and large sports drink restores energy and by 5:30, volunteers await dinner by playing games again. Dinner starts at 6 p.m. following a prayer. The cook has made oven-baked chicken, homemade noodles, and a green salad. Vegetarians enjoy burritos with beans, rice and salsa, and everyone devours ice cream cake. Humor abounds as volunteers share reports about work done, and sometimes, re-done. Reports completed, short-termers move all the dishes into soapy bins, then learn how to operate dishwashers. In short order, they finish their kitchen duties and enjoy a restful evening before turning in, this time sleeping quite well. The alarm goes off and it's time to start again.

Lofland et al. (2006) identify several additional memo types: coding, methods and analytical. Following on the importance of coding, a *Coding Memo* outlines the code, its definition, and a few examples. The memo can be written up as a word-processing file, or jotted on a note card, or embedded within a computer software system; see Box 3.3 for an example.

An *Operational/Procedural (Methods) Memo* specifies the data gathering and analysis process to date, summarizing what has been done and where the study needs to go next (see Box 3.4). A methods memo serves as a reflective process enabling the research to emerge and develop.

The final type memo is the *Theoretical Memo,* a piece that captures understanding, meaning, and—increasingly as the study goes on—richness, depth, and focus. An analytical memo becomes more and more refined as the study moves from broad to specific. Analytical memo-writing should increasingly link data to conceptual and/or theoretical understanding. The memo could also be a model or a diagram of a process that has been observed. For example, after disasters and wildfires, people generously donate a variety of items, many of which must be organized, distributed, and (often) stored, sold, or disposed of. An analytical memo of the process might look like Figure 3.1, which is in graphic form or like Box 3.5 which is in narrative form.

As such, analytical memos serve as break-through pieces that enable researchers to make sense as they gather the data and form the foundation to write up the research findings.

Box 3.3 **Initial Coding Memo**

....

Coding Memo, Late February, 2009
Victoria, Australia, Black Saturday Wildfire
Initial coding began on interviews with those who directly experienced the massive wildfire in Victoria, with a focus on survival strategies. Initial codes include:

Stay and Defend—*data indicate that survivors remained in their home or place of employment attempting to protect property as the wildfire passed. Data suggest that those who stayed and defended had training (need to verify numbers of those with fire training vs. those without).*

Leave Early—*data indicate that survivors left their property in advance of the fire's arrival and did not experience significant levels of heat or smoke while evacuating. Note to coders: estab-lish timeline for departures vis-à-vis known fire locations and fire weather. Is there a cut-off point for safe departure?*

For more examples, see: McLennan, Jim, Mary Omodei, Glenn Elliott, & Alina Holgate. 2011. "Deep Survival": Experiences of some who lived when they might have died in the February 7, 2009 bushfires. *The Australian Journal of Emergency Management* 26/2: 41–46. And: Whittaker, Joshua and John Handmer. 2011. "Community bushfire safety: a review of post Black Saturday research." *Australian Journal of Emergency Management* 25/4: 7–14.

Box 3.4 **Methods Memo: Survey Sampling**

....

Haiti Earthquake, Port-au-Prince, January 25, 2010
Travel remains difficult in the stricken capital city of Port-au-Prince. Normally a short drive, reaching the area now used as a relief camp took hours through arduous and challenging conditions. Upon arrival, the United Nations needs assessment research team decided to plot a grid over the relief camp using satellite imagery, then number the grid sections and begin gathering survey data using a random sample.

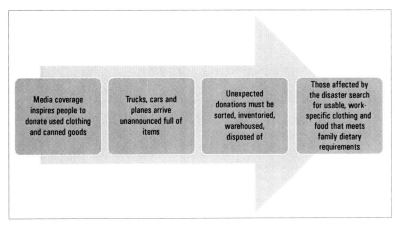

Figure 3.1 As seen in Table 3.1, data can be collected qualitatively for use in creating visual depictions of data or for data-entry into quantitative analysis programs.
Source: Based on Phillips, 2009, with permission.

Box 3.5   **Initial Analytical Memo**

....

Analytical Memo: Material Convergence
Hurricane Sandy, New York City Area, November 2012
Observations empirically verify the original work of Fritz and Mathewson (1956) who observed various forms of convergence. In the case of donations, the concept of "material convergence" clearly has occurred in the post-Hurricane Sandy context. While people need housing and furniture, they have an abundance of used clothing and canned goods. Dynes (1994) explains this abundance as a form of "situational altruism" inspired by misperceptions of need and reliance on the prosocial nature of society.

4

WRITING STRATEGIES

Overview of the Chapter

This chapter invites readers to reflectively consider how they choose to write up their findings. A number of techniques unfold in this chapter, concentrated on how social processes are revealed by QDR. Specific techniques include how to write a story using techniques that include cycles, spirals, trace-back and trace-forward approaches, sequences, and turning points. Each technique is illustrated with an example from disaster studies. The chapter then challenges the reader to "make choices" about the voice and format used in writing up research findings. A final section demonstrates how to write up a methodology section with an example drawn from disaster research.

Writing Strategies

Several good, general guides on writing up qualitative research exist (Wolcott 2008; Lofland et al. 2006; Golden-Biddle and Locke 2007; Richardson 1990). Unfortunately, advice on how to write up qualitative *disaster* research has yet to appear. In this section, we look at several models for how to write up qualitative studies and illustrate those approaches with disaster examples. Finally, this chapter provides an example of a qualitative disaster study that might be conducted based on what we have learned so far.

Writing Up Processes in QDR

As noted earlier, qualitative research has a tendency to uncover depth embedded in processes—such as the stages and steps found in post-disaster housing recovery (Quarantelli 1982), in donations management, or during debris removal. Lofland (et al. 2006) suggest that processes can be understood as cycles, spirals, and sequences. Dissertation and thesis students, aspiring journal writers, and established scholars can draw from these suggestions to organize and take their committee members or readers through an unfolding series of events. Highly descriptive, such processes rely on coded data to document elements contained within the cycles, spirals, and sequences.

Cycles

The notion of a cycle is based on a "recurrent sequence of events which occur in such order that the last precedes the recurrence of the first in a new series" (Lofland et al. 2006, p. 152). Think of a cycle as one that occurs repeatedly, such as the four phases in the life cycle of emergency management. Though ideally emergency managers want to put themselves out of work, the reality is that activities fall into an expected, repeated sequence: preparedness, response, recovery, and mitigation. Though the stages do not neatly conform to a cycle, to a specific time of day or year (like holidays), and do tend to overlap (Neal 2004), in general we can distinguish between four phases. Nor is the United States the only location to do so. In New Zealand, the four "R's" appear in cyclical fashion: readiness, response, recovery, and reduction.

Emergency operations plans (EOPs) can be viewed as a cycle, too. Ideally, planners work with stakeholders (emergency managers, elected officials, first responders, voluntary organizations, government agencies, citizens) to design a plan. An EOP should be viewed as a "living document" that changes over time, becoming more attuned to local hazards, available resources, and response capabilities. Triggering mechanisms for the cycle would include training people on the plan (remembering that people forget or leave, and need to be replaced), tabletop and full-scale exercises, and actual events. Post-exercise or post-disaster, a "hot wash" should occur where stakeholders honestly review incident management and improve the EOP through active revision. The cycle then starts again, with training, exercising and activation.

Spirals

What distinguishes a cycle from a spiral is that spirals are not as stable as cycles. Rather, spirals are a "continuously spreading and accelerating increase or decrease" (Lofland et al. 2006, p. 153). Stakeholder interest in mitigation increases and decreases over time, with the highest levels of interest occurring after a disaster has happened. Often called the "window of opportunity," mitigation planners find the post-disaster phase to be the time when people are most willing to agree to mitigation changes, such as elevations, policy initiatives, or buying insurance (e.g., Kunreuther 2006). Interest usually wanes as people move away in time from the event and prefer to use household income for other pressing needs.

Weather can also occur in spirals. Drought represents such a spiral. In the state of Oklahoma in the United States, for example, drought conditions in the 1930s generated the "Dust Bowl" where massive dust storms buried houses, caused deadly respiratory conditions, and devastated the largely agricultural state. Returning drought conditions in 2010 to 2013 reduced water supplies significantly, causing communities to launch water restrictions and lay in new infrastructure to bring in water from nearby communities. Data from the Oklahoma Mesonet supports the returning conditions:

The impacts to Oklahoma agriculture and water have been severe. The latest "Oklahoma Crop Weather Report" from Oklahoma's office of the USDA's National Agricultural Statistics Service finds 88 percent of the state's topsoils and 94 percent of its subsoils rated in poor or very poor condition. One year ago, those values were at 63 percent and 91 percent, respectively. The report also noted 73 percent of the state's pasture and rangeland in poor or very poor condition. The portion of the Oklahoma wheat crop rated poor or very poor rose from 12 percent to 30 percent over the last week. The damage done to the topsoil became evident on Oct. 19 when strong winds lifted dust across Interstate 35, dropping visibilities down to zero in a *scene reminiscent of the historical Dust Bowl storms* [emphasis added]. The shroud of dust caused a chain reaction wreck of as many as three dozen vehicles. Eleven of the state's major reservoirs are at less than 70 percent of capacity, up from just three at the beginning of May. Lake Altus is in the worst shape at 17 percent normal capacity. Canton Lake, an important part of Oklahoma City's water supply chain, is at 42 percent. (Oklahoma Mesonet 2012, see http://www.mesonet.org/index.php/news/article/oklahoma_drought_continues_to_expand).

Related drought conditions include fire weather, which might seem seasonal but is not. Though wildfire tends to break out worst in the late spring and summer (March through September) in Oklahoma, conflagration can occur at any time of year. On January 28, 2013 (normally the colder winter weather), the National Weather Service issued a "Fire Weather Day" alert based on temperature, humidity, drought, and wind.

Researchers interested in other topics besides weather might think of firefighters and other first responders negotiating for benefits. It is likely that efforts to increase pay, health care, retirement options, and disability would see increases and decreases as tensions rise and ebb, lobbying efforts expand and fall off, and public support swells and wanes. Post September 11th, for example, studies began to document lingering and deadly effects of exposure to toxic elements at Ground Zero and the Pentagon (Landrigan et al. 2004; Herbert et al. 2006). Problems with respiratory problems, called the "World Trade Center Cough," led to efforts to fund special programs for those affected, primarily first responders. The U.S. Congress changes its composition every two years due to the election cycle. Bills can languish, which was the case for those seeking health care after September 11th. Initial efforts failed to pass federal legislation. A second effort resulted in a filibuster with one party blocking the other party's efforts to move the bill forward. Eventually, President Obama signed the bill in January 2011—nearly ten years after the attacks. Known as the James Zadroga 9/11 Health and Compensation Act, the legislation memorializes the first police officer verified to have died from exposure at Ground Zero.

Sequences

For sequences, Lofland (et al. 2006) indicate that scholars should think of steps or stages in time, not unlike the career/chronology aspect of the C Model (Quarantelli 2002). Disasters typically mark a place in time when things changed (Neal 2013), offering a point of departure—but in which direction? Lofland and colleagues indicate that three possibilities exist for aspiring writers: the trace-back technique, trace-forward option, and turning points. Other choices include presenting the process, offering a life history, or presenting the data in an analytical manner (Erlandson et al. 1993).

Trace-Back Technique

In the trace back technique, writers identify the disaster in time and space. For example, on January 12, 2010, a massive 7.0 magnitude earthquake struck Haiti. Much of the capitol city, Port-au-Prince, and surrounding areas sustained massive damage as buildings pancaked. As many as 250,000 people may have died. Hundreds of thousands more sustained serious injuries that caused disabling and lingering health conditions. A trace-back technique would start from January 12, 2010 and work backwards in time. What conditions led to the massive loss of life? Investigations since the earthquake have pointed to the nation's lack of building codes to create seismically-resistant structures.

Others point to long-standing and deeply embedded political, economic, and social problems that led up to the event. Political turmoil has destabilized the nation repeatedly for hundreds of years. Prior to the earthquake, the United Nations had established the United Nations Stabilization Mission in Haiti (MINUSTAH), in a building that collapsed in the earthquake, killing critical mission staff. Economically, Haiti's profound impoverishment had led to selling local resources externally, including trees needed for food, fuel, furniture, and building. As deforestation increased, rural populations pushed into the capital city area in search of work and a means to feed their families. Extremely high levels of debt to foreign nations resulted in an externally dependent political economy.

Limited funds meant that minimal police, firefighting, and emergency management resources existed within the government and that ordinary citizens had no means to protect themselves from risk. From a trace-back technique, the tragedy in Haiti occurred because of challenging structural conditions that fostered high levels of human vulnerability.

Trace-Forward Technique

The trace-forward approach works in the opposite chronological order. An event occurs, and researchers investigate the consequences as they unfold minute by minute, hour by hour, or day by day. Documents such as EOC logs or WebEOC data help to relate the story, as do personal accounts gathered through interviews. Johnson (1988) analyzed police interviews with survivors after a massive fire broke out in the Beverly Hills Supper Club near Cincinnati Ohio in 1977. His data clearly showed that most people died in twos and threes, usually within their own dining group. Johnson's research showed that people remain socially loyal despite significant risk and impending death.

In a study of deaths that occurred prior to a music concert in Cincinnati, Johnson (1987) found that people went to extraordinary efforts to help people remain upright as a large crowd compressed tightly toward the concert venue. People within the crowd passed others up and overhead in an effort to save lives as people began to suffocate. His study revealed that the open-seating policy needed to be repealed. Because the first arrivals secured the best seats, a large crowd had gathered. Unfortunately, the building doors opened outward into the crowd, which meant that people had to step back, causing the compression. Personnel within the building did not realize that people pushing into the doors were fighting for their lives, and some assumed that staggering crowd members were drunk or disorderly—rather than oxygen-deprived. From the point of opening the doors through the arrival of ambulances and medical personnel, eleven people perished.

On January 27, 2013, a fire broke out in a crowded nightclub in Santa Maria, Brazil. Estimates suggest that 2,000 people inside sought rapid exit through one door staffed by security guards.

Some fell, others tripped, and exiting became even more problematic. Guards thought that rowdy college students were fighting or attempting to leave without paying and blocked their departure. From the time that the fire broke out to the heroic efforts of concert-goers re-entering the doorway to pull others to safety, approximately 230–240 people died, or about 11% of the entire crowd. The majority died from smoke and toxic fume inhalation. A trace-forward approach would begin with the moment musicians used pyrotechnics during their concert to the culmination of the tragic event, identifying key points in the time sequence as perceived by those interviewed, from video cameras, or from documents such as police and firefighter reports.

Turning Points

Retrospective accounts also focus on turning points that lead to significant changes. Certainly, September 11th resulted in world-wide changes. In the United States, FEMA merged into a newly-established Department of Homeland Security which pulled 22 total federal agencies under its new mission. Federal allocations also changed, funding response efforts that focused on attacks including chemical, biological, and radiological hazards. New language emerged, including the terms "soft targets" such as subways, public malls, and water treatment plants. New jobs developed, with the U.S. Federal Aviation Administration (FAA) hiring armed federal air marshals to secretly safeguard the air traveling public.

Other examples abound, with the critical aspect being to determine the turning point and its effects. What is key is that things change after the turning point, and they could change for the better or the worse. The change in homeland security funding in the United States, for example, brought in badly needed response resources for many fire and police stations. However, emergency managers pointed out that the most frequently occurring hazard was a flood—a natural event, not a terrorist event—with diminishing means to conduct flood mitigation projects.

As another example of a turning point, hurricanes Camille and Betsy slammed into the U.S. Gulf Coast states in the 1960s, causing extensive loss of life and physical damage. Faith-based and community based organizations (FBOs/CBOs) sent funding and volunteers into affected areas trying to alleviate pain and suffering. Once there, they realized that their efforts overlapped and that they could better utilize their resources. To do so, they created the National Voluntary Organizations Active in Disaster (NVOAD) group, which still serves as an umbrella-type organization under which FBOs and CBOs coordinate their work. In the decades that followed, many participating NVOAD members developed specialties and expertise in given areas. The Seventh Day Adventists, for example, typically organize warehouses for storage and distribution of donations. The Church of the Brethren provides qualified and credentialed child-care workers (Peek, Sutton and Gump 2008). NVOAD thus became a centralizing means for discussion of unmet needs and a vehicle through which members could identify problems and design solutions. After the 1993 Mississippi River flood, which damaged dozens of states, NVOAD partners tackled the difficult donations issue by working with FEMA to design a donations management guideline (see http://www.nvoad.org/library/cat_view/8-donations-management).

Turning points can be identified as large-scale moments in time (September 11th) in which noticeable changes occurred. But micro-level changes can be identified as well. The moment when a disaster survivor moves from their stricken city to a new, permanent location represents such a turning point. In that new location, they learn to navigate physically, socially, and culturally. They make new friends, find new work, and move away from the disaster's impact on their lives—or, perhaps they do not. Perhaps they find racism, lack of work, and marginal housing (Weber and Peek 2012). Maybe the disaster has separated them from loved ones and they disappear into the horrors of human trafficking (Fisher 2010). Turning points may seem like the macro-scale moments that capture our collective attention, but helpful insights for theory and practice can be gleaned from a micro-level inquiry as well.

Reveal the Process

Qualitative disaster research generates much understanding about various processes. A process can be understood as a series of stages and steps that people, organizations, communities, and even governments go through. Classic studies suggest that people move at varying rates through sheltering and housing (Quarantelli 1982a and 1982b). Similarly, the process of donations management has increasingly built on processes that involve taking in unsolicited as well as requested donations, sorting and organizing the donations, and finding ways to move donated items out to those in need.

Writers can use identified processes as a framework around which to present data. Written cases can describe steps chronologically or topically, but usually a stepwise approach reveals the key moments that separate human activities, reveal degrees of organization and inter-organizational coordination and collaboration (or the lack thereof), and lead readers toward outcomes and explanations.

Consider, for example, the process of debris removal. Multiple steps can be discerned:

- Communities conduct pre-disaster debris management planning and identify leadership, departments, and procedures.
- The disaster happens, with debris strewn and comingled across the community.
- The local community requests and receives help and funding from various governmental agencies.
- Local officials initiate contracts with debris removal companies and establish oversight procedures.
- Local leaders conduct public education efforts to explain the process of sorting debris into appropriate piles for green waste (trees, bushes), white goods (appliances including refrigerators that must be taped shut due to rotted food), recyclables (that can be donated or resold), and construction/demolition materials (that can be incinerated).
- Appropriate vendors and departments begin debris removal, focusing first on roadways to allow for emergency transport.
- Debris moves to sorting locations into recyclables, resellables, reduction (incinerate), mulching (green waste), and permanent disposal.
- Local officials conduct oversight of debris operations to insure that fraud does not occur under contracts.
- The community begins to return to normal.

Debris removal also requires the establishment of curbside sorting, coordinated pickups, temporary sites for management of various kinds of waste, incineration locations, and permanent landfills.

In short, research questions will likely drive the choices that you will have to make about writing up your disaster research. "How" questions (how did people regain their housing) reflects more of a process question. "When" (when did people evacuate?) questions likely lead writers to choose turning points. Time periods and the availability of data may also influence what you can and cannot do. It may be impossible to secure information that has perished about the recent past, directing one's attention toward what happened since (and thus a trace-forward approach). What is most important is to make a mindful choice over writing up one's data.

Making Writing Choices

Qualitative studies can be written up as technical reports, empirical journal articles, edited collections, or full-length volumes like books, theses, and dissertations. Journal articles usually rely on predictable sections (Erlandson et al. 1993). The author begins by discussing the problem under study along with its significance to the discipline or practical field. Such an initial section usually also addresses the research questions, assumptions and limitations of the study. A review of extant literature then follows, although some qualitative researchers prefer to place related studies toward the end of an article, as an aid to interpret the findings and to avoid biasing the reader. A methodology section then follows, which in journal articles may be rather abbreviated due to space limitations. Books, theses, and dissertations always include well-developed methodology sections, although publishers may ask book authors to place research design information in an appendix. Methods sections typically include discussion of the sample population, the methods or procedures, development of the instrument, data analysis processes, and techniques that enhance the credibility and trustworthiness of the data. A richly developed descriptive section then follows in which authors present the findings. Various forms to present findings can be used including those presented earlier: domain, taxonomic, and componential analyses; typologies; themes, categories or major codes; or C models or similar frameworks. Each presentation is substantiated with illustrative data such as the carefully coded quotes, field note excerpts, visual images, or documents. Memoranda pay off here, as they often form the basis for interpretations presented by the authors. Finally, authors work through the implications of their work—do the findings confirm, negate, or inform the extant literature? What conclusions can be drawn for policy and/or practice? What limitations affected the study? What should future researchers focus on in order to further the body of knowledge on this subject?

In this section, we work through choices that authors must make as they begin to develop and frame their work, beginning with making an informed choice about "voice."

About "Voice"

Prospective authors must make choices about how to present their data as well as the style in which they will write. Rather than sitting down and simply spilling out the content, wise authors make informed choices rather than following standardized approaches. For example, many students follow academic tradition when they first begin to write up qualitative data, with a common approach being to use second person. In qualitative research, it is acceptable to use first person ("I observed, We interviewed") which may feel awkward at first. However, using first person fits consistently with feminist and post-modern choices to acknowledge the multiple realities present in the study, including the voice of the author.

Feminist scholars, and qualitative researchers in general, compel us to let the emic perspective emerge in our writing. When writing up the content, we must let the subjects' voices and perspectives be heard. Usually, a narrative style walks the reader through the data, using interview quotes, field note excerpts, visual data, or documents that reveal the lived experience of those who participated in the study. Do not be afraid to include multiple quotes to illustrate a key finding. Doing so takes the reader inside the participants' lived experience. Think of the quotes as comparable to a table of statistical data found in a quantitative article. Presenting your data enables readers to make assessments of the credibility and trustworthiness of your data (more on this later).

About Format

Much of qualitative research relies on the traditional case study format (Lincoln and Guba 1985; Yin 2008). Several writing styles can be considered (Yin 2008; for theoretical storytelling, see Golden-Biddle and Locke 2007):

- *Linear-Analytic.* Here, the author clearly identifies a problem under study, lays out the methodology and findings and presents conclusions and implications. Such efforts can be explanatory, descriptive, or exploratory. Linear-analytic studies reflect more traditional academic presentations, which can be quite successful when publishing qualitative work in historically quantitative journals. Webb (2004) used archival data from the Disaster Research Center to look at the ways in which responders improvised their roles during various disasters. One might think that responders and emergency managers step into familiar roles and carry out prescribed duties. However, Webb's stepwise analysis uncovered five types of role improvisation that involved procedural, status, normative-order, equipment, and location/facility changes.
- *Comparative Structure.* In a comparison, the author repeats the case study format several times in order to demonstrate insights and similarities across the cases. Studies that emanate from explanatory, descriptive, or exploratory purposes fit this model. Fordham (1999b) compared two cases in which a working-class and a middle-class community faced flooding. Her in-depth interviews, ranging from three months after the event to four years later, demonstrated that disasters are not equal opportunity events. Other differential responses also appeared, requiring that professionals develop a greater understanding and sensitivity to how gender stratification influences response and recovery. Fordham's comparison revealed that communities needed additional

empowerment over disaster management in order to reveal and address emerging needs.

- *Chronological.* Information in this format presents in historical order, which may be helpful in identifying influential conditions that appear as an event unfolds. Again, these formats can be explanatory, descriptive, or exploratory. Perry and Lindell (1997) used the traditional case study format to discuss relocation in an Arizona community. Sometimes contested, relocation decisions mean permanent removal of people to a new location and away from familiar places and even people. In this case, a successful relocation happened—but how? The story unfolds chronologically as we learn that intensive interaction between citizens and officials led to the eventual multi-year process of moving an entire town to a safer location. From interviews and documents, Perry and Lindell document and explain the importance of citizen-centered involvement in decision-making around such a life-altering situation.

- *Theory-building.* In each section of a theory-building case study, the author works to unravel a part of the theoretical argument being made. Useful for explanatory and exploratory work, the theory case study relies on data to enrich understanding of existing concepts or to introduce new ideas. Kreps and Bosworth (2006, p. 299;) reported on dozens of case studies to identify and explain the complex ways in which groups and organizations "restructure to meet disaster demands." Their complex analysis revealed that varying structural forms appear in varying contexts, from completely emergent groups to highly structured organizations.

- *Suspense.* Interestingly, authors who opt for the suspense format reveal the ending at the beginning. Unraveling something like a murder mystery, the reader knows that the murder has occurred but does not know who did it or why. Explanatory case studies rely on suspense formats. Studies of mass fatalities have been presented in this manner, with the author revealing that lack of building codes, inadequate response capabilities, weakened political structures, gendered stratification systems, open-seating or limited exiting and similar conditions resulted in the numbers of deaths (Johnson 1987; Scanlon 2006).

- *Unsequenced.* Usually descriptive, an unsequenced case study does not rely on a particular order, but the content must be complete in its presentation. An unsequenced study usually focuses on topics central to a research question. For example, Lowe and Fothergill (2003) interviewed people who volunteered after September 11th in the United States, revealing their findings thematically: initial reactions to the attacks, motivations to volunteer, and the impacts of volunteerism. Lowe and Fothergill then explained volunteer behavior through the concept of convergence, in which personnel (volunteers) move to a scene to help. Their study led to recommendations for proactive engagement of these often-spontaneous volunteers.

Sample Methodology Section

The purpose of the following section is to illustrate how a methodology section might be written up for a qualitative disaster research project. The section reflects content from previous chapters in a manner designed to organize ideas around a central research question. As you read through this section, think of a research project that you have in mind. How can you use the sections, sub-sections, and approaches described here to craft a research project of your own?

The Research Question

People are motivated to help those affected by disasters. Without prompting, unsolicited numbers of volunteers often converge on damaged areas. Well-intentioned, these "spontaneous unsolicited volunteers" (or SUVs) often present a management problem to communities already struggling to conduct emergency response activities. Conceptually, SUVs can be subsumed under a phenomenon identified as convergence behavior (Fritz and Mathewson 1957b; Lowe and Fothergill 2003; Rodriguez, Trainor, Quarantelli

2006). SUVs are conceptually distinct from experienced and trained volunteers associated with and credentialed by disaster response organizations (Drabczyk 2003; Dyregrov et al. 1996; Britton 1991).

Several forms of convergence occur in a disaster setting including material (donations) and personnel (volunteers) convergence. Without advance planning to anticipate volunteers' arrival, those eager to serve may go away un-used and frustrated. In contrast, communities hosting such SUVs will need to manage the altruistic spirit of those converging to leverage the social capital they produce for response and—especially—during the recovery period when extensive volunteer assistance is often needed more than during the immediate response time period (Airriess et al. 2007). In short, communities and organizations typically need to plan for and adapt to mass personnel convergence (Flint and Stevenson 2010; NVOAD, no date; Sutton 2003).

The three-fold purpose of this study is to follow the life-span of a personnel convergence event, to understand why such behavior occurs, and to identify strategies for managing the convergence. The overarching research question is: How do recipient communities manage personnel convergence to leverage the immediate and long-term use of such social capital? Central to answering this main question are additional foci: (1) what motivates SUVs to converge on a disaster scene; (2) how do local communities and/or organizations manage the arrival and dispersal of unsolicited aid; (3) how do volunteers perceive their service; (4) how do both volunteers and communities/organizations volunteers experience failures to use converging assistance; (5) to what extent do local communities and/or organizations maintain relationships with volunteers for long-term recovery purposes?

An Inductive Approach

Although a considerable amount is known about volunteerism (e.g., see Wilson 2000 Musick, Wilson and Bynum 2000), research on disaster-time volunteerism remains surprisingly minimal (for examples see Franke and Simpson 2004; Lowe and Fothergill 2003; Peek, Sutton and Gump 2008). Given the dearth of such research on personnel convergence during crisis occasions, an inductive, holistic and naturalistic approach is merited. Inductive research pays attention to initially-collected data to make sense of what the researcher is hearing and seeing. The general questions will serve as initial foci, which will allow for unanticipated but important questions to appear as data are gathered.

To do so, the research team will spend one day gathering data by conducting preliminary interviews and observations. Using semi-structured interviews and by crafting mini- and grand tours of places that volunteers move through (from arrival at the disaster through work assignment sites), researchers will capture a "day in the life of a volunteer." This day will then be reviewed by the research team during a debriefing session the evening of the first day of data-collection. A flow-chart of volunteer movement will be developed initially, resulting in a set of working hypotheses. These hypotheses will reflect upon the first two research questions and reveal initial impressions on what motivates convergent volunteers and how they enter and move through (or leave) the disaster scene. Subsequent data collection will re-examine these stages in the process of managing SUVs to determine if those stages remain intact, alter over time (and under what conditions), and with what impacts. The working hypotheses will be refined as the data confirm, negate, or otherwise modify how volunteers and volunteer managers manage and researchers understand the lived experience of volunteers.

Working Hypotheses

Qualitative research relies on working hypotheses that emerge inductively as data are gathered and analyzed. Specific to what is already known in the research literature, several initial working hypotheses can be discerned (see above):

- The majority of those arriving will report they came based on media reports that raised their concerns and motivated them to assist.
- The majority of those arriving will not have called in advance to check if they were needed.
- The majority of those arriving will have food and water for one day of service and will not have plans for securing additional food inside the damage area—or for a place where they will stay overnight.
- The majority of those arriving will not have any affiliation with experienced disaster organizations.

- The majority of those arriving will not have any prior disaster experience or training in disaster response.
- More men than women will volunteer in the hardest-hit areas. Work will be divided on a gendered basis, with men being more likely to use power tools and heavy vehicles.
- More younger than older volunteers will serve in the hardest-hit areas, particularly in locations that require heavy lifting.
- It is assumed that homeowner and volunteer experience may differ based on their proximity to the hardest-hit areas. A working hypothesis is that volunteers working in areas of most significant damage will find their work more meaningful than those from the outer fringes where less damage occurred.
- The community and affected organizations will not have a pre-designated volunteer management plan.
- Volunteer managers will use newly-crafted information forms, new locations for action, and new personnel to manage the influx of SUVs. Volunteer management will thus be characterized as emergent in nature.

Ethical Considerations

Disaster settings tend to generate high levels of altruistic response. Despite the devastation, volunteers are eager to help. Residents affected by the disaster, despite common myths, are typically ready to pick up the pieces and start the journey toward recovery. Most disaster victims, in fact, do not suffer from the stereotypical disaster syndrome that suggests that victims are psychologically devastated. Most disaster victims, in contrast, respond fairly well and draw upon previous experience, social networks, and personal resources to begin recovery. Those who manage volunteers may vary from experienced emergency managers to local volunteer coordinators to those who lack experience with disasters and/or volunteers. Those who manage may thus experience the influx of volunteers along a continuum from those they expected and are ready to deploy as critical resources to those who overwhelm local capacity.

Researchers should thus be sensitive to a range of emotional and psychological reactions that might occur. Ethical researchers will anticipate both the risks and benefits associated with conducting research on these groups and in a disaster setting. The type of disaster may matter as well. Terrorist events, for example, are intended to provoke psychological and emotional pain and researchers should be sensitive to such matters. Technological events, such as a nuclear plant accident, may prompt blaming behavior which places the researcher in a set of contentious actors with potential legal implications for the data collected. Even natural disasters may spark angst, such as that seen after Hurricane Katrina when accusations of government incompetence surfaced rapidly.

Ethical considerations relevant to the potential setting include several types of risks and benefits to the prospective participants. *Risks* to the participants may include:

- Loss of time the volunteer or manager intended to devote to victims.
- Potentially embarrassing questions or feeling that their altruistic intents were being questioned.
- Loss of confidentiality given a low-level but potential breach in security purposes.
- Capturing visual images that reveal people, places, or behaviors that may be considered private.

Benefits may include:

- Sharing one's story.
- Contributing to the science of disaster studies and to improvements in volunteer management (Newman and Kaloupek 2004).

To manage these risks, researchers will ask subjects to review and sign an informed consent form that spells out the risks, benefits, and procedures that will be undertaken in the study. It is assumed that individuals will "have the capacity to provide meaningful and voluntary informed consent to participate in research" (Collogan et al. 2004, p. 369; Rosenstein 2004). Subjects will be advised they have the right to:

- Decline to participate in the study.
- Refuse to participate in any dimension of the study without penalty.
- Refuse to answer any question without penalty.

- Review a transcript of their interview for corrections.
- Be instructed to ask for permission before taking any photographs and to secure the names and contact information of those in the photos.
- Be interviewed at a time and place of their preference.
- Receive contact information for the researchers and their institution's IRB.

Sampling

Three main groups of individuals will need to be sampled. The first group, arriving volunteers, will be chosen based on their arrival at fifteen-minute increments. Those volunteers will be provided with a camera for visual documentation of the "typical day in the life of an SUV." A matrix will be kept to insure that a wide range of volunteers will be able to record their experiences. Variation by gender, age, race, and ethnicity, and distance traveled will be ensured (Musick et al. 2000). If possible, the matrix will be compared to any volunteer database that might be amassed by the host community. The second group will be officials in charge of receiving, processing, managing, training, dispersing, supervising, and debriefing volunteers. These officials may include those who serve as emergency managers or volunteer coordinators, or come from community-based organizations, emergent groups, or the faith-based sector. To delimit the sample, only those involved in managing the arrival of unsolicited volunteers will be included. Officials or organizational leaders who arrive with pre-trained, experienced response teams (such as Mennonite Disaster Service or Southern Baptist Disaster Relief) will be excluded. The third sample will include recipients or beneficiaries of volunteer service such as homeowners, business owners, or similar individuals. To select those individuals, a spatial zone sampling strategy will be used including individuals from the immediate impact zone where most damage has presumably occurred, the next semi-concentric zone where less damage has happened, and the outer zone where minimal damage is evident (Killian 2002).

Setting(s)

Three types of settings are anticipated, all of which should prove rich sites for data collection. The first setting is assumed to be a point of collection for arriving volunteers and is often called a Volunteer Reception Center (NVOAD, no date). In similar events, such locations have included a local college (Joplin, Missouri in 2011), and a local coliseum (Fort Wayne, Indiana, 1982). The researchers will station themselves in a place where they can capture mini- and grand tours of the setting. The grand tour will describe the overall area and designated locations for action within that setting (Spradley 1980). The grand tour will depict how people move through the locations for action to capture the flow of how local authorities manage and convert human capital into leveraged resources for response. The mini-tours will describe (in detail) specific locations for action. For example, a sample mini-tour will enable a reader, auditor, or advisor to "see" a table where arriving volunteers register for service and are then sent further into the volunteer center for subsequent training and deployment. The people, forms, clipboards, files, computers, pens, pencils, whiteboard, markers, and/or other types of materials at the registration table will be described in detail. By doing so, the reader will be able to see not only the process of registering volunteers but the resources and personnel who begin the process of transforming eager volunteers into work teams with specific assignments.

Methods

Four main methods will be used to capture data: interviewing, participant observation, documents, and visual data. Doing so will ensure that a triangulated data collection procedure will take place to enhance credibility and trustworthiness of the data.

Interviewing. Interviews will be conducted using semi-structured interview guides for the three populations (Rubin and Rubin 2012). First, a guide will be constructed to capture the motivations of arriving volunteers, the manner in which their day of volunteerism unfolds, and the meaning of their service. Second, an instrument will be designed to ask volunteer managers about what they did to move volunteers from arrival through registration, orientation, training, and assignment (as relevant). This instrument will be focused on the steps and stages of volunteer management as it unfolds. Should a pre-disaster volunteer management plan exist, the document will be collected and compared to what actually transpired. Should emergence characterize the volunteer management process, the process that appears will be discerned through initial interviews and then confirmed through subsequent and/or follow-up interviews. Third, homeowners who become beneficiaries of volunteer service will be interviewed for their thoughts on the service that was provided and the meaning it generated in their lives.

The inductive process requires that the instrument will transform over the course of the research as revealed through the preliminary data analysis process. To illustrate, nightly debriefings will enable the research team to determine how the process has changed and the reasons for such alterations. It is anticipated, for example, that volunteers will increase over time and then peak at some point. It is thus additionally anticipated that volunteer managers and centers will need to adapt by expanding and contracting accordingly (Sutton 2003). The division of labor, and locations for action inside the volunteer center, as one illustration, will likely change as well. Interview guides will need to adapt to capture these rapidly-unfolding dimensions of volunteer management. As a consequence, understanding and depiction of volunteer management will be richer and deeper (Geertz 1973).

Participant Observation. The research team will use a range of observational strategies from complete observer to complete participant (Spradley 1980). These varying roles offer perspectives that yield insights from the outside of a setting to the inside. At the onset, observations will be conducted to gather grand and mini-tours of the volunteer management center, various locations for actions inside the center, and exterior work sites in and around the disaster scene. In addition to this complete observer role, participant observation will also be conducted. Several members of the research team will present themselves as volunteers in order to experience the volunteer management process directly. At least one member of the team will move through the process to the worksites and spend time helping on a disaster site. Another member of the team will volunteer to help at the volunteer coordination center. They will take jotted notes as possible and then develop their experiential notes into full field notes each night of the field study (Lofland et al. 2006).

Site selections are typically based on several criteria (Spradley 1980). First, since the vast majority of disaster research is conducted by social scientists, an observation site must contain specific social elements, namely a place where social actors and social activities take place (Spradley 1980, p. 39). Anthropologist James P. Spradley suggests that researchers think about *kinds* of places to launch an inquiry. For the purposes of this study, *kinds* of places are likely to include: arrival places (parking, registration); volunteer coordination places (registration, training, transportation); worksites (streets, homes, businesses, parks); and volunteer needs (bathrooms, eating facilities, first aid sites, places to sleep). Similarly, kinds of actors should also be considered. In this setting, kinds of volunteers are expected to include a range from novices to experienced; volunteer managers should also range from emergent to pre-designated and from inexperienced to knowledgeable. Homeowners should also be thought of in various categories as well, from those who are able to help alongside volunteers to those who cannot (at work, caring for children or are children, injured by the storm, elderly, those with conditions that prevent participation, or even kinds of families, age ranges or genders). Activities also fall into a diverse array of behaviors. It is anticipated that activities will eventually fall into predictable and routine patterns of recognizable behaviors which increasingly move volunteers from the chaos of arrival to the application of their skills and abilities in appropriate settings.

Documents. Any pre-disaster volunteer management plan will be collected. Such a document will enable the researcher to compare and contrast the lived reality of a personnel convergence event with the community's pre-event planning. Communities capture data on volunteers in various ways. Depending on the community, they may record volunteer information electronically or on straightforward sign-up forms. Should that be the case, the research team will negotiate with the community to view the volunteer data in order to identify demographic trends including gender, age, skills, hometown, distance traveled, and other data as captured by the local community. Newspapers articles, flyers, posters, and other documents will be gathered as they are found or uncovered. Increasingly, social media are used to attract, direct, and record volunteer experiences (Hovey 2007). These social media (e.g, Facebook, Twitter) will be reviewed as documentary data and will be collected as well.

Visual Data. Multiple ways to gather visual data will be conducted for multiple purposes, which helps to generate an emic perspective (Rose 2007; Banks 2007; Collier and Collier 1986). The means by which visual data will be gathered will be used for photo-elicitation and photo-documentation from both insider and outsider perspectives. To capture insider perspectives, digital cameras will be provided to arriving volunteers who will be instructed to "record your volunteer experience as it unfolds." Cameras will be provided to the person who steps up to the volunteer coordination point at fifteen-minute intervals. As an alternative, individuals wanting to use their own camera phones (David 2010) will receive a pre-paid gift card to compensate for providing their photo album on their day. Doing so will insure a randomness among those who receive the cameras. Individuals will be instructed to return the camera at the end of their shift and will receive a DVD/flash drive with their photos on it. They will then be asked to participate in an interview about their volunteer experience by describing every n^{th} photograph they took. To start the photo-elicitation strategy, they will be asked to give each photograph a title and then to explain why they gave it that title. Should volunteers be too exhausted to participate, they will be asked to provide contact information so they can participate in a follow-up interview. The photographs will be matched to the location where the photo was taken. Within 24 hours, a member of the research team will visit the site and attempt to contact the individual(s) who lived or worked in the setting. Photo-elicitation interviews will then be conducted with the homeowner, business owner or other appropriate representative (Harper 2002). They will be asked to give a title to selected photographs and to describe what they saw. Should they be unavailable due to the impact of the disaster, up to three contacts will be made to try and include their participation.

A second means of visual data collection, photo-documentation, will be used as well. This data collection procedure directs the researcher to capture themes that reveal themselves during an event. An initial strategy is to conduct photo-saturation by recording data thoroughly. Standing in the center of a volunteer reception center, for example, will serve as an initial strategy. It is likely that a process of meeting, greeting, organizing, and dispatching volunteers will occur. Photo-documentation will record those process-based steps and stages as well as apparent deviations that unfold.

Social media (described above) also include visual imagery. Community-based sources of social media (such as Facebook pages) will be reviewed for the images that are posted. A thematic analysis of these self-selected documents will be conducted. Attempts will be made to follow up with the organizations or individuals who posted the images to determine why they chose to post those images.

Data Analysis Procedures

Grounded theory, a classic data analysis approach, will be used to analyze transcription and observational data (Glaser and Strauss 1967). Data analysis will proceed from the onset of data collection (Lofland et al. 2006). Initial efforts will involve research team members in open coding to surface key categories of meaning within the data. A constant comparative process will be used in concert with the open coding to ensure that consistency occurs when determining placement of the coded data within the open codes. Two researchers will work in concert on the open coding process to facilitate naming of the open codes, the boundaries of the codes, and the degree of agreement over the coded content. On every third transcript, the researchers will present their initial findings to the larger research team for discussion, thus generating a consensus on the open codes and their content.

The research team will collectively identify promising codes that could serve as a signal category of meaning. To illustrate, a category of meaning might emerge from the data, such as "retrieval efforts." Coders will then engage in selective coding to focus in on the category and identify properties and dimensions (Strauss and Corbin 1990). Properties represent various aspects of the category, such as the level of effort that volunteers make to retrieve homeowner possessions in the debris field or "value perceptions" regarding the worth of the item being retrieved. Selective coding will then reveal dimensions of the properties. For example, the property of value perceptions might be dimensionalized along a continuum from social value to economic value. Although additional coding (e.g., axial) might be conducted by the research team, the "quick response" nature of the project requires that findings be unearthed expeditiously in order to leverage findings for additional grant funds. It is anticipated that the exploratory and emergent findings uncovered through this classic grounded theory approach will result in a more robust research proposal for the larger grant proposal.

Credibility and Trustworthiness of the Data

Although the project is based within a quick response framework, efforts will be made to enhance the credibility and trustworthiness of the data (Lincoln and Guba 1985). Triangulation, or the use of multiple methods focused on a single study, will allow for confirmation of findings. For example, coded findings between transcriptions and observations should be consistent. Peer debriefings will serve as the main technique while in the field gathering data. Researchers will gather every evening to discuss preliminary impressions and work to focus the project appropriately, per the expectations of a naturalistic paradigm. Key interviewees will be invited to review their transcripts and preliminary findings for their input, which is a classic member check.

Every fifth transcription or observational session will be set aside for referential adequacy. Setting these materials aside serves as a technique useful for verifying findings. By not examining these materials until after the coding has been completed, they serve as a reference check that can verify or negate the findings. Similarly, the team will engage in negative case analysis in which they search actively for observations contrary to the main findings and then become engaged in resolving those variations.

Another technique central to this study will be the use of a research team. Because team members provide varying perspectives, a fuller range of viewpoints and observations are likely to result. Reconciling any differences they observe will strengthen the data by focusing the team in on common patterns versus deviations from those patterns. The research team coordinator will maintain an audit trail for examination by the principal investigator as an additional check on the credibility of the findings (see more in the next chapter on this topic).

5

EVALUATING QUALITATIVE DISASTER RESEARCH

Overview of the Chapter

How do you evaluate qualitative disaster research findings? This chapter will pick up an earlier thread on writing up your findings, but in the context of how others might evaluate your work. A significant section of this chapter addresses how you can convince readers of the trustworthiness and credibility of your scholarship. A detailed section outlines the use of audit trails and the role of an outside auditor. A concluding section will address how to evaluate both basic and applied research specifically for disaster research, policy-making, and practice.

Issues of Trustworthiness and Credibility

Quantitative research relies on techniques designed to improve the reliability and validity of the data analysis and rely on the generalizability of their research to produce useful results. Qualitative researchers use different terminology than reliability, validity, and generalizability. Instead, qualitative scholars use the terms trustworthiness, credibility, and transferability (Lincoln and Guba 1985). In short, what qualitative researchers attempt to do is to answer questions about whether or not their data collection and analysis procedures realistically portray the social setting.

Perhaps what concerns most critics is the issue of transferability. Quantitative techniques that rely on small samples to represent larger populations are powerful. The data produced through probability samples during elections, for example, can enable researchers to state who will win. Critics often charge qualitative researchers with an inability to leverage their samples to such a broader representation. But such charges are inherently false in nature because they miss the intent of qualitative studies: to produce rich, deep insights into social settings, processes, and interactions. By generating thorough, nuanced, and often complex renderings of social settings and human interaction, qualitative analysts allow readers to judge for themselves about the transferability of the content.

Imagine, for example, an insider view of being a shelter resident. After Hurricane Katrina, researchers found that residents hoarded food, to the chagrin and concern of shelter managers who saw the behavior as inappropriate (Pike, Phillips, Reeves 2006). While the extent of food security across all shelters and displaced populations remained unknown, realizing why people hoard granola bars and bottled water is certainly transferable to other settings. What emerged as important to understanding socio-behavioral response in the shelters was the context in which the hoarding occurred. For people previously stranded on rooftops, overpasses, and flooded neighborhoods, their food security issues were very real—and represented a means to re-establish psychological comfort for themselves and their families.

Nine different techniques enable qualitative disaster researchers to increase further the trustworthiness and credibility of their data collection and analysis processes. These nine techniques, while not unique to disaster research, appropriately address a number of challenges associated with such inquiry. This section first reviews and defines the nine techniques, then outlines ways in which the measures enable researchers to deal with—and even overcome—issues discussed previously. To begin, the techniques used most often to increase credibility and trustworthiness of the data include (Lincoln and Guba 1985; Erlandson et al. 1993):

- *Triangulation.* Probably the most commonly-used qualitative research technique to establish trustworthiness and credibility in disaster research is triangulation. The process means that investigators focus in on a research question from various methods using a combination of observation, interviewing, archival research, and visual analysis. These different vantage points enable the researcher to compare and contrast what has been written (such as on an emergency operations plan) with what is said (during an interview). Deviations suggest points to follow up on and often yield meaningful insights for theory and practice (e.g., people do not always follow the plan, leading to improvisation; Kendra and Wachtendorf 2006).
- *Prolonged engagement.* The idea of prolonged engagement means staying in the social setting for a long period of time. Preferably, the researcher will remain until they are not observing any new patterns of behavior and can predict with some accuracy what social interactions or processes will occur. The length of time this will take can vary considerably and probably depends on the degree to which the researcher has gained entrée, established rapport, and become something of an insider. Ideally, prolonged engagement means that people drop their front stage behavior so that a researcher can determine how people really behave (Goffman 1959).
- *Focused and persistent observation.* Along with prolonged engagement, researchers must increasingly focus their attention on an aspect of the research setting. Social settings produce multiple perspectives that must be understood to produce an accurate, detailed, and informative study. Settings also offer many angles of investigation. However, not every element, despite its intriguing qualities, can be studied. Choices must be made to narrow the study. By doing so, the researcher can attend increasingly to the details that enrich understanding and generate theoretical advances.

Persistence means that researchers remain patient and engaged. Staying in or frequently returning to the setting enables the researcher to capture the setting realistically.

- *Research teams.* Perhaps one of the most valuable techniques available to disaster researchers is the use of research partners. Given the debates previously discussed over the insider-outsider point of view, involving several team members in any single study is a good idea. Barriers to insiders erected by age, gender, perceived ability, or occupation may exist. Unfortunately, most researchers have failed to integrate disaster practitioners onto their research teams. Increasingly, as disaster sites are wrapped up by security, researchers are having difficulty negotiating access. Involving disaster practitioners is a good idea to assist with entrée, moving past gatekeepers, and establishing rapport. In addition to the obvious contributions that true insiders can make regarding research questions, their credibility with other professionals make them a valuable addition. Further, the combination of insider and outsider on a research team increases the chance that team members will capture and understand native language, non-verbal behavior, and other subtle but critically important elements of a social setting. Insiders help researchers with that elusive emic perspective so vital to qualitative research.
- *Peer debriefers.* Colleagues, team members, and even insiders to a setting can serve as people to turn to when assessing one's work. The purpose of peer debriefing is to offer an unbiased perspective on how field work develops and is written up. Peer debriefing also functions as an early form of peer reviewing, which usually occurs after a scholar submits a manuscript to a prospective publisher. Rather than rely on such late reviews once the writing has been completed, peer debriefers visit with the researcher about their research questions, methodological procedures, field work issues, and preliminary findings. Peers can prompt researchers to think more deeply about the data and to make more complex linkages across the research effort. Debriefing may be particularly important in an unfamiliar setting. During research

on a faith-based organization managing volunteers
after Hurricane Katrina, for example, I turned to fellow
disaster researchers at the University of New Orleans.
Discussions generated deeper insights into how coastal
cultures and communities had evolved, survived, and
interacted with outsiders arriving to help. The debriefing
sessions fostered a greater confidence in how I interpreted
what local people said. As one example, an interviewee
remarked, "Everyone is invited to help, but *few* are invited
to gumbo." Debriefing shed light into the extent to which
the faith-based organization had successfully entered and
interacted with cultures distinctly different from their
own. Lessons learned resulted in a set of best practices
when outsiders make entry to beleaguered communities
struggling to determine who they can trust.

- *Member checks.* Somewhat similar to peer debriefing, a
member check occurs when the researcher returns data
or reports to human subjects for their review. Such data
might include interview transcripts or summaries on
which the subject can correct or reflect. Similarly, initial
reports can be reviewed for their accuracy and the extent
to which they ring true to real insiders. At early stages,
such a member check can discern misunderstandings
over language, behavior, or context, and redirect the
researcher back to a more trustworthy path. Researchers
may discover differences of opinion as well, and will
need to reconcile those issues. Contrasting views, for
example, may indicate a need for the researcher to
verify perceptions, to expand the sample, and/or to
find ways to honor the multiple and overlapping views
inherent in any social setting. Although member checks
may seem time-consuming or expensive in the case of
producing carefully-rendered transcripts, the value of
such effort (and related funding) increases the accuracy
of the research product. Given limited funding, it may
be feasible to ask a carefully-selected and representative
sample of subjects to participate in the member checks.
In my own research on Katrina, I discovered errors that
varied from my own spelling of local cuisine and jargon.
Reconciling these discrepancies, while time-consuming,

ultimately made the final products less embarrassing and far more accurate.

- *Audit trails.* An audit trail operates much like a set of accounting books in that it records daily transactions—such as methodological decision-making, interview guides and updates, working hypotheses, raw data, preliminary memos, coding strategies, data analysis, and initial reports. The idea of an audit trail (see below) is to create a path by which an outside auditor (such as a colleague, consultant, or professor) can review the research process and determine if raw data leads inductively to findings and interpretations.

- *Referential adequacy.* When analyzing qualitative data, coding procedures reduce the data into themes or categories. How does a researcher ensure that they did not miss a theme or how do they gain confidence that their findings resonate across all of the data? Referential adequacy occurs when the researcher sets aside a portion of the data for later analysis. For example, if a researcher collects thirty interviews, she can set aside five of those for later review. Those five can be chosen at random, such as setting aside every fifth interview. The analysis then proceeds using the techniques described earlier. After completing her coding, she organizes the coded data into a domain, taxonomic, or componential analysis (Spradley 1980). Then, she looks back at the interviews that were set aside to see if the same coding procedures result in a similar—or a different—analysis. As an alternative, the researcher can ask a peer or an auditor to review those set-asides vis-à-vis the analytical products. The same can be done with observations, documents or visual data. Consistency between the original twenty-five and the set-aside five increases the trustworthiness of the findings. Inconsistency suggests an extensive review of the analytical products. In short, the set-aside transcripts serve as a reference to check the adequacy of the findings.

- *Negative case analysis.* In the final technique, the researcher looks vigorously for instances, behaviors, cases, procedures, or processes contrary to the findings. The point of any negative case analysis is to identify the extent to which the data have produced a consistent picture and the boundaries or extent of that picture. Negative cases do not necessarily undermine the analysis but may point the researcher toward those with divergent opinions or procedures within the social setting. Imagine, for example, that a long-term recovery committee works closely with faith-based organizations in a given community. Interviews document that the majority of the time, faith-based organizations send representatives to attend case management meetings for prospective clients who need homes rebuilt. Such patterns persist across ten of twelve communities. In two of those communities, participation by outsiders lags at the case management meetings. Discerning why that variation occurs enriches understanding when subsequent investigation to resolve the discrepancies uncovers poor leadership, conflict, or lack of resources.

Audit Trails

One highly-recommended practice to enhance credibility and trustworthiness of research findings is the use of an audit trail (Lincoln and Guba 1985). The function of an audit trail is to lay a path for an outside auditor to review research from data collection through data analysis and findings. Audit trails present data in an organized manner so that the auditor, much like a financial accountant, can follow the research process from beginning to end. Ideally, that process will demonstrate visible linkages between the data and the conclusions so that the auditor will conclude that results have been grounded firmly in the data rather than influenced by the researcher's bias. An audit trail ensures that the voices of participants yield rich, deep insights illuminating the social setting and producing substantive knowledge, theoretical insights, evidence-based practices, and sound policy recommendations. The auditor and the audit trail collectively document credibility of the study.

Several general principles should guide development of the audit trail. To start, the audit trail should be easy to move through, meaning that it should be organized carefully and thoughtfully. Although software programs can be used to do this, a set of materials external to the software program is advisable. In most studies, additional material may accumulate that may not be incorporated into the software. For example, a researcher might import only transcriptions and leave important memos, observational notes, sampling information, and other key material out of the software. For this reason, it is a good idea to organize an electronic and/or hard copy audit trail. Always back up your electronic copies, including any software files and products.

The format of such a trail varies and can be electronic, hard copy, or both. The trail can be organized in a notebook or set of connected file folders. Regardless, the primary rule is to organize it. To aid the auditor, a table of contents should be produced with page numbers, clearly identified sections, and an explanation of how to follow the data from collection to writing up the results. Common elements of an audit trail include the following.

A *Methods Section*—that presents and/or discusses:

- Your fieldwork proposal.
- Information from any funder.
- Ethical concerns and IRB materials.
- Site selection(s) and related issues.
- Discussion of safety issues as relevant to the study.
- Reflective memos on issues and context specific to disaster studies.
- Information on entrée, gatekeepers, and sponsors.
- Sampling approaches and outcomes.
- Discussion of insider/outsider status and roles.
- Consideration of the ways in which you developed and maintained relationships with research participants.
- Credibility and trustworthiness of the data (see below).

Data Section (as relevant for the methods that you have deemed appropriate):

- Overview of the methods that you chose and your justification.
- Informed consent letters with signatures (being sure to follow protocol to safeguard confidentiality, which may require separating such letters from the data).
- Instruments (all of them, including revision notes).

- A glossary or dictionary of terms and jargon specific to your setting.
- Field journal documenting daily work undertaken.
- Raw field notes (jotted, full).
- Interviews (notes and transcriptions).
- Observational notes (written up for use in analysis).
- Documents (with an inventory list) linked to source (e.g., archive, organizational files).
- Photographs and videos (with an inventory list); explanation of visual techniques in use.
- Memos (methods, analytical, theoretical).

Analytic Section (links back to the data):

- Codebook with explanation of the codes.
- Coding (links to analytical section, the audit trail); explanation of coding scheme.
- Figures (e.g., domain, taxonomic, or componential analyses from early efforts to polished products).
- Explanation of the way in which the data links through coding to the analytical products like domain analyses so the auditor can follow the trail.
- Discussion of emerging themes from coding, memos, etc.
- Discussion and presentation of more detailed findings (e.g., from selective coding).

Ideally, the auditor should be able to trace a finding back through the analytical process to the original data, such as the interview transcript or observational notes. Computer software programs can facilitate this process, as most record the number or pseudonym on the transcription or notes and carry it over to the coded excerpts organized in a set of codes (also called a report). The trail produced by the software should allow an auditor to determine if the codes, categories, themes, or figures (e.g., domains, taxonomies, and componential analyses) are firmly grounded in the data. A line of thought (e.g., these data support personnel convergence) should be clearly discernible so that the auditor will trust that a rigorous process has been applied.

Finally, who should serve as an auditor? For a student, the thesis or dissertation advisor and/or committee members serve that function. For professionals, a colleague with expertise in qualitative disaster research would suffice or even a consultant paid as part of a research grant. In general, always select someone experienced in conducting qualitative disaster research so that they understand the challenges, context, and procedures.

What most researchers new to the use of an audit trail find difficult is the process of linking the data. It is relatively easy, for example, to simply place the above-listed items in the trail. Demonstrating their linkage can be more difficult. Fortunately, software packages have made this process easier and can be reproduced by those who prefer more traditional analytical processes. Some products that can help demonstrate linkages include:

- Raw data, including original transcripts. Auditors are likely to use these as references during their analysis. A written explanation can help the auditor to move through the trail. Ultimately, the explanation and the audit trail will also help you, the researcher, when you return to the data to publish results. Qualitative studies can take years to produce, so an audit trail can help your memory too.
- Printouts of themes identified during the data reduction process. These can include reports generated by a software package that identify who was speaking (i.e., the number or pseudonym of the interviewee). For example, a report produced by NVivo or ATLAS.ti on a theme like "Volunteer Highlights" will also identify the interview transcript from which it came. The auditor can then return to that interview to determine how well the data fits with the theme and be sure that the reference culled from the interview data truly fits into the theme of "Volunteer Highlights."
- Memos that write up the themes in narrative fashion, with references to the reports that were generated (perhaps by telling the auditor the name of the printout and where to find it in the audit trail). The auditor should be able to read the memo, look back to the software report printout, and then find the ideas firmly grounded in the interview transcript.

- Preliminary writings that will eventually turn into thesis, dissertation, or book chapters or journal article sections can then be presented. The auditor should clearly see linkages between the preliminary writing, the memo, the analysis and the data. The data trail should be clear from data collection through analysis to writing up the findings.

The use of an outside auditor is key because the majority of journals do not allow sufficient space to explicate the qualitative data analysis process. Auditors confirm your credibility, the soundness of your approach, and—ultimately—your reputation in the field.

Evaluating Written Products

Dissertation and theses committees, journal reviewers, book editors, and publishers all look carefully at the written products to determine their viability for publication (see Box 5.1 and Box 5.2). Certain standards exist across all disciplines and certainly apply to qualitative disaster research. In addition, QDR also merits additional review due to the unique context in which it occurs.

Expectations for Qualitative Research

A number of authors have provided sound advice on writing up qualitative research (e.g., Golden-Biddle and Locke 2006; Wolcott 1995; Richardson 1990). Implicit within many of their views is a set of expectations for good qualitative research (Silverman 2010). Essentially, reviewers or committee members will look for how well the research design and methods fit the research question. For example, if a researcher wants to understand how closely an organization followed their emergency plan, then some combination of written records (plans, EOC data, reports) coupled with first-hand interviews and observation should be included.

Authors are also assessed on their own abilities to present and critique their methodology (Silverman 2010). All studies have issues and credible authors present any problems that arise, their efforts to address them, and the impacts they have on the study. Honesty is part of being scientifically responsible, and acknowledging the problems inherent within any field study must occur. Methods must be laid out systematically so that reviewers can make an assessment of the quality of the effort as well as the quantity of the data.

Critiques must also be made of the data analysis process: Was it a standard approach? Did the author follow the specified techniques? Was the approach selected the best one to produce a credible and trustworthy result?

Finally, reviewers of QDR will look to its impact. Did the author either situate the work in the relevant empirical findings of the field or use them to interpret their results? Did the author either rely on agreed-upon concepts to interpret the data or convincingly produce new concepts grounded in the data? Theoretically, is the work reflective of interpretative lines of thought in the field? Or, is the piece sufficiently strong enough to support a new or revised theoretical stance? Qualitative disaster research has been critiqued as "atheoretical," as in lacking a theoretical positioning and interpretation. Increasingly, reviewers will expect that theoretical perspectives will either influence QDR or be produced by researchers (McEntire 2004).

Bring the Emic Perspective

Perhaps surprisingly, you may write in the first person with approval from your graduate committee or the journal or book editor. However, prospective authors should be aware that most journals prefer a third-person voice unless the journal publishes work from ethnographic or qualitative traditions. Using the first voice honors a reflexive tradition in qualitative research to acknowledge one's presence and influence on the setting and the research participants.

Qualitative research also should allow for the emic perspective to show through, which means presenting the voices of those present in the research settings. Readers should be able to move inside the lived experiences of those affected by disasters and understand their perspectives. Why were they on the roof after the flood? Why did they not evacuate? Good qualitative disaster researchers allow for the perspectives of rooftop survivors to be told so that readers can understand the context.

In Box 5.1, Dr. Lori Peek offers some good suggestions regarding development of qualitative research for a book chapter or any

Box 5.1   **Writing a Qualitative Disaster Research Book Chapter**

Lori Peek is co-editor of *Displaced: Life in the Katrina Diaspora*, author of *Behind the Backlash: Muslim Americans after 9/11*, and co-author of *Children of Katrina*.

1. ***Follow the rules of good writing.*** When writing up qualitative research—any research, for that matter—authors should strive to reach the widest audience possible. As such, the research problem, methods, data, findings, and conclusions should be clearly and thoroughly described. A well-organized chapter or article should offer a compelling narrative and include effective and descriptive headings and strong topic sentences. Writing in the active voice is almost always preferable to the passive. Following the basic rules for good academic writing is essential!

2. ***Emphasize the strengths of qualitative research.*** Qualitative researchers tend to seek to gain new insights, to understand the meaning that people assign as they make sense of their lives, to reveal complex phenomena and social structures, and/or to give voice to those who are rarely heard. As such, the best qualitative research offers thick, rich description that centers on the voices of the participants and engages all of the readers' senses. When I've finished reading my favorite ethnographies, I could envision the participants in my mind's eye and I could hear their voices. When authors achieve that kind of depth and richness in their writing, they rarely go wrong.

3. ***Use figures or other graphic representations to represent findings.*** Although rich description is the hallmark of qualitative research, scholars who make the most lasting contributions often make analytical and theoretical contributions as well. This means that qualitative data are presented in such a way that they suggest new hypotheses or concepts, reveal social processes as they unfold over time, or offer a typology of categories or characteristics. Once the hard work of analyzing and

writing up all the textual data has been completed, authors should attempt to represent the findings graphically. This will help the reader to more quickly grasp the key contributions and hopefully to retain those contributions over time.

4. ***Be explicit about your research methods and techniques of analysis.*** Most qualitative research textbooks, rightfully so, emphasize that the qualitative researcher is the "primary instrument" of data collection. Because data are mediated through the researcher, rather than through close-ended questionnaires, for example, it is all the more important that authors be explicit about their role in the setting, the time spent in the field, the content and quality of data collected, and the ways that those data were analyzed.

5. ***Leave time for reflection and feedback.*** No writer produces perfect prose on the first pass. As such, it is critical that authors leave enough time to read, review, and revise their own work. It is also preferable that all authors seek out feedback from trusted colleagues, mentors, or editors. The feedback received will likely help further improve the arguments and narrative flow of your work. Good luck, and happy writing!

qualitative disaster research manuscript. A strong thread throughout her own work, as well as her advice, is to ensure that the voices of insiders become prominent. As mentioned throughout this book, reviewers of qualitative disaster research require that authors take them inside the lives, organizations, neighborhoods, and communities, or the strategies, processes, and experiences that disasters produce. Readers should leave your manuscript having moved mentally inside the experiences of those you studied. They should hear the emic or insider perspective and feel that they leave your work with a greater understanding of what happened and why. As readers, we should be able to explain to someone else—based on your work—the events and their meaning. Good qualitative research brings the emic perspective to the forefront by developing a strong and informative narrative that tells a story.

Writing Specifications

A critical part of submitting any journal article or book chapter involves following the submission specifications (see links to sample journals below). Editors and reviewers will expect that a qualitative disaster scholar will submit a carefully written and edited manuscript (Becker and Denicolo 2012). Each journal will also specify their standards regarding length, sections (often with headings and sub-headings), and references. Footnotes or endnotes may be permitted or not. References will need to be formatted in a specific manner. Figures and tables will also need to be formatted and placed per the directions of the publisher. Journals may also specify the language in which the manuscript must be submitted, such as in English but with British spellings.

Submissions should always be scrutinized by authors for deviations from what specific journals allow and what editors expect. Deviations may result in rejection or, at best, a "revise and resubmit" from the editor. Failing to follow the specifications will result in an elongated time from initial submission to publication. In short, follow the directions. In Box 5.2, Dr. Eve Coles offers good

---

Box 5.2   Criteria for Evaluating Qualitative Research

Eve Coles is the editor of Emergency Management Review, and an experienced researcher and educator in the field of disaster studies. In this boxed feature, she discusses what she looks for in qualitative disaster research as a journal editor and as a reviewer for other journals.

When I am reviewing papers that have used a qualitative approach to their research and data collection I look for the following things:

1. **Transparency and Credibility**: The first thing I am looking for is a clear disclosure and description of all the relevant research processes. Authors must use established qualitative data collection methods and analytical processes. Or, if the author uses a novel process, it should be described and justified. I am also looking for some credibility in the form of the research focus/question and how it lends itself to qualitative research, such as

well-grounded contextualisation, triangulation of the data, and a good set of references.

2. **Philosophical and Theoretical Underpinning**: Secondly, I would like to see the theoretical stance of the researcher(s) clearly stated. This means that authors should present a clearly framed conceptual framework. Their framework needs to be underpinned by evidence from the literature review. Submissions should state a clear ontological and epistemological position.

3. **Sound Understanding of the Context**: Thirdly, I want to know everything there is to know about the subject of the research: the how, what, where, when and why of the "action." I expect to see a demonstrated, strong understanding of the context of the research that is substantiated by appropriate evidence/literature that is both broad and balanced in its outlook.

4. **Methodology**: Next, I am seeking a clear set of aims and objectives and an indication of what the researcher(s) hopes to discover in their investigation (including their assumptions), how they will achieve it (the research design) and how it will confirm or extend the knowledge.

5. **Ethics**: Lastly and certainly not least (particularly where disaster research is concerned), I am looking for some detail of the ethical considerations given to the research process and how such considerations were dealt with in the investigation.

advice on what she expects as editor of *Emergency Management Review* (http://www.epcollege.com/epc/knowledge-centre /emergency-management-review/).

Dr. Coles' expectations are consistent with other editors as well. For example, Dr. Maureen Fordham served as the first (and, to date, the only) woman to edit the oldest journal in the field, the *International Journal of Mass Emergencies and Disasters* (www.ijmed.org). Dr. Fordham (2013) encourages writers to "respect the originator of the textual material you are using. For example, do not practise extractive research which only takes and does not give back or repay in some way." Such a philosophy is consistent with feminist perspectives discussed earlier in this book: that we must respect how people entrust us with their experiences and perspectives. As authors, we must remain ethically bound to practice a norm of reciprocity that redistributes the equity in the researcher-participant relationship. Second, Dr. Fordham suggests that we should make efforts to "try to personalize or humanize your participants; for example, give them names/pseudonyms rather than numbers when you use extracts from their transcriptions." Authors must make choices when presenting their data, and the use of pseudonyms (to protect confidentiality) can give a face to an otherwise coldly de-identified human being. Third, she suggest that authors must craft their writing honestly so that they are "true to the meaning of the participant and do not decontextualize to the extent that you misrepresent them." Qualitative disaster research must always be situated in the context in which it occurred, which provides insights on the time, place, and circumstances that influenced options, actions, and interactions. Fourth, we should always practice the highest ethical standards in our writing. To do so, Dr. Fordham recommends that we "consider the impact of the extracts you are using; try to avoid publishing anything that potentially humiliates whilst still maintaining the veracity of the original material. For example, often people speak ungrammatically and there is a temptation, for the best reasons, to 'clean up' or correct the text to avoid readers' contempt. However, it is better to consider this 'ungrammatical' text as a form of dialect which is integral to the participant's identity and to keep it in its original form." To do so, a member check is usually a good option to make certain that you have accurately recorded the sound of the dialect correctly.

Journal Specifications

Prospective authors must determine if the journal will accept qualitative research and if so, what type of publication. Some journals prefer classic empirical works while others invite theoretical or policy pieces. Being sure that your manuscript fits with the intent and scope of the journal will save heartache. Authors must prepare manuscripts consistently with the specifications for various journals, or the work will not be reviewed well or sometimes not at all. Examples of journal submission expectations can be found at these links (last accessed March 31, 2013):

- *International Journal of Mass Emergencies and Disasters,* http://www.ijmed.org/article-submission/.
- *Environmental Hazards,* http://www.tandfonline. com/action/authorSubmission?journalCode=tenh20&pag e=ins tructions#.Uiu7Rz8k_iU.
- *Journal of Contingencies and Crisis Management,* http://onlinelibrary.wiley.com/journal/10.1111/%28I SSN%291468-5973/homepage/ForAuthors.html.
- *Journal of Emergency Management,* http://www. pnpco.com/pn06012.html.
- *Disasters,* http://mc.manuscriptcentral.com/disasters.
- *Disaster Prevention and Management,* http:// www.emeraldinsight.com/products/journals/ author_guidelines.htm?id=dpm.

Dealing with Rejection

Qualitative disaster researchers may publish in disaster-specific journals or in discipline-specific journals. Toward the latter, it is advisable to provide contextual information on the way in which QDR occurs. Discipline-specific journals often lack reviewers familiar with the challenges of conducting disaster studies. There are several strategies for avoiding such a demise for your manuscript.

First, it is acceptable to write a letter to the editor of the journal explaining how you conducted your research and the ways in which it fits with established techniques in the field. Although the methods section should be sufficiently strong to convince reviewers of the rigorous methods that you undertook, an additional overview letter highlighting your methodological strengths is a good idea.

Second, take the time to develop the methods section. An editor or reviewer can always request a more concise version of your methods for the final publication. But taking the time to explain, situate, and substantiate your methodology is important. Not all reviewers appreciate or understand qualitative studies and by taking the time to explain your approach, you may avoid a negative review.

Third, if you experience a rejection (from a committee or a journal), take the time to breathe. Wait until you can sit down calmly and review the comments. Take their comments seriously, as the reviewers (or committee members) probably put a great deal of time and thought into what they said. Consider their points of view, questions, confusion, or suggestions seriously. Then, work on revising and resubmitting. The time that you take to do so will likely result in a better manuscript and increase your chances of publication.

Finally, do revise and resubmit your work. Most authors do not have their work accepted the first time that they submit it to a committee or to a journal. Too many good manuscripts languish or never become part of the body of knowledge on a given topic because authors fail to follow through with revisions. In short, get used to rejection and accept that revision is part of the process of publishing scientific work (Becker and Danicolo 2012).

Publishing Your Work

Though it may take time to produce the manuscript that a journal will accept or a dissertation that a committee may approve, the effort is worth it. No one runs a marathon successfully without taking the time to train for it. A lot of trial and error occurs with such training: learning what to eat or not to eat, dealing with injuries, slogging through energy-deprived runs, and sometimes having to pull out of the marathon and try again later. Qualitative disaster research is not unlike the marathon. We must train appropriately by acquiring strong methodological skills. Personal trainers can help as well, and novices should rely on committee members, mentors, editors and reviewers for guidance. One does not prepare for the marathon overnight, instead it is a time-consuming process. It is a good idea to have a strong base, or several years of running experience, before diving in. The parallel here is spending time in classes, reading qualitative disaster studies, researching in the field, following a mentor, and working with qualitative data at your computer. As successful marathoners know, the first twenty miles of the 26.2 miler are the easiest. It's the last 6.2 miles that really require that you dig down deep inside and go the distance.

The same is true with publishing qualitative disaster research. We must put in the time to get across the finish line successfully. It is incumbent, then, on all of us to do so. The scientific integrity and rigor of our work matters, because it contributes not only to the body of knowledge in our disciplines but also to policy and practice. People's lives—our family members, our neighbors, and our community associates—depend on our faithfulness to the research process.

REFERENCES AND ADDITIONAL READINGS

Albrecht, Gary L. 1985. "Videotape Safaris: Entering the Field with a Camera." *Qualitative Sociology 8*: 325–344.

Airriess, C et al. 2007. "Church-based social capital, and geographical scale: Katrina evacuation, relocation and recovery in a New Orleans Vietnamese American community." *Geoforum 39*: 1333–1346.

Babbie, Earl. 2010. *The Practice of Social Research*. Belmont, CA: Wadsworth.

Baca Zinn, Maxine. 1979. "Field Research in Minority Communities: ethical, methodological, and political observations by an insider." *Social Problems 27*: 209–219.

Ball, Michael S. and Gregory W.H. Smith. 1992. *Analyzing Visual Data*. Newbury Park, Ca: Sage.

Banks, Marcus. 2007. *Using Visual Data in Qualitative Research*. Thousand Oaks, CA: Sage.

Barton, Alan. 1970. *Communities in Disaster*. NY: Anchor.

Becker, Howard. 1981. *Exploring Society Photographically*. Chicago: University of Chicago Press.

Becker, Howard. 1978. "Do Photographs Tell the Truth?" *Afterimage 5*: 9–13.

Becker, Lucinda and Pam Denicolo. 2012. *Publishing Journal Articles*. Newbury Park, CA: Sage.

Becker, Howard. 1975. "Photography and Sociology." *Afterimage* Special Issue (May-June).

Bell, Holly. 2008. "Case Management with Displaced Survivors of Hurricane Katrina." *Journal of Social Service Research 34*: 3, 15–27.

Blinn, Lynn M. 1987. "Phototherapeutic Intervention to Improve Self-Concept and Prevent Repeat Pregnancies among Adolescents." *Family Relations* 36: 252–257.

Blinn, Lynn and Amanda W. Harrist. 1991. "Combining Native Instant Photography and Photo-Elicitation." *Visual Anthropology 4*: 175–192.

Blocker, T. Jean and Darren E. Sherkat. 1992. "In the Eyes of a Beholder: Naturalistic and Technological Interpretations of a Disaster." *Organization and Environment 6/2*: 153–166.

Bogdan, Robert and Sari Knoll Biklen. 1992. *Qualitative Research for Education.* Boston: Allyn and Bacon.

Boldt, Kelly and Timothy White. 2011. "Chilean Women and Democratization: entering politics through resistance as Arpilleristas." *Asian Journal of Latin American Studies 24*(2): 27–44.

Britton, Neil. 1991. "Permanent Disaster Volunteers." *Nonprofit and Voluntary Sector Quarterly 20/4*: 395–415.

Bucher, Rae. 1957. "Blame and Hostility in Disaster." *American Journal of Sociology 62*: 467–475.

Burby, Raymond, Ed. 1998. *Cooperating with Nature.* Washington D.C.: Joseph Henry Press.

Burgess, Robert G. 1982a. "The Unstructured Interview as a Conversation." In Burgess, Robert, (Ed.), *Field Research*, pp. 107–110. London: George, Allen, and Unwin.

Burgess, Robert G. 1982b. "Elements of Sampling in Field Research." In: Burgess, Robert, (Ed.), *Field Research*, 76–78. London: George, Allen, and Unwin.

Chetkovich, Carol. 1997. *Real Heat: Gender and Race in the Urban Fire Service.* New Brunswick, NJ: Rutgers University Press.

Clive, Alan, Elizabeth Davis, Rebecca Hansen and Jennifer Mincin 2010. "Disability." In: B. Phillips, D. Thomas, A. Fothergill, L. Pike (Eds). *Social Vulnerability to Disaster*, 187–216. Boca Raton, FL: CRC Press.

Comfort, Louise. 1996. "Self Organization in Disaster Response: the Great Hansin, Japan Earthquake of January 17, 1995". Quick Response Report #78, University of Colorado Natural Hazards Center.

Collogan, Lauren K., Farris Tuma, Regina Dolan-Sewell, Susan Borja and Alan R. Fleischman. 2004. "Ethical Issues Pertaining to Research in the Aftermath of Disaster." *Journal of Traumatic Stress 17/5*: 363–372.

Collier, John Jr. and Malcolm Collier. 1986. *Visual Anthropology: Photography as a Research Method.* NY: Holt, Rinehart and Winston.

Crowe, Adam. 2012. *Disasters 2.0.* Boca Raton, Florida: CRC Press.

Cutter, Susan. 2006. "The Geography of Social Vulnerability." Available at http://understandingkatrina.ssrc.org/Cutter/, last accessed March 31, 2013.

Curry, Timothy J. and Alfred C. Clarke. 1977. *Introducing Visual Sociology.* Dubuque, IA: Kendall/Hunt.

Cutter, Susan. 2002. *American Hazardscapes.* Washington D.C.: Joseph Henry Press.

Dash, Nicole, Brenda G. McCoy, and Alison Herring. 2010. "Class." In: Phillips, B., D. Thomas, A. Fothergill, L. Pike. *Social Vulnerability to Disaster*, 101–122. Boca Raton, FL: CRC Press.

Dash, Nicole, Betty Hearn Morrow, Juanita Mainster and Lilia Cunningham. 2007. "Lasting Effects of Hurricane Andrew on a Working-Class Community." *Natural Hazards Review 8*: 13–21.

David, Gaby. 2010. "Camera Phone Images, Videos and Live Streaming." *Visual Studies 25/1*: 89–98.

Drabczyk Anne L. 2003. "Ready, Set, Go: Recruitment, Training, Coordination, and Retention Values for All-hazard Partnerships." *Journal of Homeland Security and Emergency Management 4*: Article 12.

Deegan, Mary Jo. 1990. *Jane Addams and the Men of the Chicago School, 1892–1918*. New Brunswick, NJ: Transaction Books.

Denzin, Egon and Yvonne Lincoln, editors. 1998. *The Landscape of Qualitative Research: Theories and Issues*. Newbury Park, CA: Sage.

Desmond, Matthew. 2009. *On the Fireline: living and dying with wildland firefighters*. Chicago: University of Chicago Press.

Diekman, Shane T., Sean P. Kearney, Mary E. O'Neil, and Karen A. Mack. 2007. "Qualitative Study of Homeowners' Emergency Preparedness: experiences, perceptions, and practices." *Prehospital and Disaster Medicine 22(6)*: 494–501.

Disaster Research Group. 1961. *Field Studies of Disaster Behavior: an inventory*. Washington D.C.: National Academy of Science, National Research Council Publication #886, Disaster Study #14.

Drabek, Thomas E. 2002. "Following Some Dreams." In: Methods of Disaster Research, Robert Stallings (Ed.), 127–156. Philadelphia, PA: Xlibris/International Research Committee on Disasters.

Dyregrov, A., J. Kristoffersen, and R. Gjestad. 1996. "Voluntary and professional disaster workers: similarities and differences in reactions." *Journal of Traumatic Stress 9/3*: 541–555.

Dynes, Russell R. 1970. *Organized Behavior in Disaster*. Lexington MA: Heath Lexington Books.

Dynes, Russell R. 1994. "Situational Altruism: Toward an Explanation of Pathologies in Disaster Assistance." Preliminary Paper 201, Disaster Research Center, University of Delaware.

Dynes, Russell R., E. L. Quarantelli. 1992. "The Place of the 1917 Explosion in Halifax Harbor in the History of Disaster Research: The Work of Samuel H. Prince." Preliminary Paper #182, Disaster Research Center, University of Delaware.

Eichler, Margrit. 1980. *The Double Standard*. NY: St. Martin's Press.

Eisenman, David P., Deborah Glik, Richard Maranon, Lupe Gonzales, Steven Asch. 2009. "Developing a Disaster Preparedness Campaign Targeting Low-Income Latino Immigrants: Focus Group Results for Project PREP." *Journal of Health Care for the Poor and Underserved 20/2*: 330–345.

Enarson, Elaine. 2000. "We Will Make Meaning out of This: Women's cultural responses to the Red River Valley Flood." *International Journal of Mass Emergencies and Disasters 18/1*: 39–64.

Enarson, Elaine and Betty Hearn Morrow. 1997. "A Gendered Perspective: the Voices of Women." In: Peacock,Walter Gillis, Betty Hearn Morrow, and Hugh Gladwin (Eds.), *Hurricane Andrew*, 116–140. Miami, FL: International Hurricane Center.

Epstein, Roby Jayaratne and Abigail J. Stewart. 1991. "Quantitative and Qualitative Methods in the Social Sciences." In: Cook, Judith and Mary Margaret Fonow, *Beyond Methodology*.

Erlandson, David A. et al. 1993. *Doing Naturalistic Inquiry: a Guide to Methods.* Newbury Park, CA: Sage.

Fine, Gary Alan, Ed. 1995. *A Second Chicago School? The Development of a Postwar American Sociology.* Chicago: University of Chicago Press.

Fisher, Henry W. 1998. *Response to Disaster*, 2nd ed. Lanham, MD: University Press of America.

Fisher, Sarah. 2005. *Gender Based Violence in Sri Lanka in the After-math of the 2004 Tsunami Crisis.* United Kingdom: University of Leeds, Master's Thesis.

Fisher, Sarah. 2009. "Sri Lankan Women's Organisations Responding to Post-tsunami Violence." In E. Enarson (Ed.), E. & Chakrabarti, P., *Women, Gender and Disaster: Global Issues and Initiatives*, 233–249. New Delhi, India: Sage Publications Limited India.

Fisher, Sarah. 2010. "Violence Against Women and Natural Disasters: findings from Post-Tsunami Sri Lanka." *Violence Against Women 16/3*: 902–918.

Fleischman, Alan R. and Emily B. Wood. 2002. "Ethical Issues in Research Involving Victims of Terror." *Journal of Urban Health 79/3*: 315–321.

Flint Courtney and J. Stevenson. 2010. "Building Community Disaster Preparedness with Volunteers: Community Emergency Response Teams in Illinois." *Natural Hazards Review.* 2010: 11.

Fonow, Mary Margaret and Judith A. Cook (Eds). 1991. *Beyond Methodology*. Bloomington, IN: Indiana University Press.

Fordham, Maureen. 1999a. "Participatory Planning for Flood Mitigation: Models and Approaches." *Australian Journal of Emergency Management*, 13/4: 27–34.

Fordham, Maureen. 1999b. "The Intersection of Gender and Social Class in Disaster: Balancing Resilience and Vulnerability." *International Journal of Mass Emergencies and Disasters 17/1*: 15–36.

Fordham, Maureen. 2013. Personal Communication with the author.

Fordham, Maureen and Anne-Michelle Ketteridge. 1998. "Men Must Work and Women Must Weep: Examining Gender Stereotypes in Disaster." In: Enarson, Elaine and Betty Hearn Morrow (Eds.), *The Gendered Terrain of Disasters: through Women's Eyes*, 81–94. Miami, FL: Florida International University.

Fothergill, Alice. 2004. *Heads Above Water: Gender, Class and Family in the Grand Forks Flood.* Albany, NY: SUNY Press.

Franke, Mary and David Simpson. 2004. "Community Response to Hurricane Isabel: an Examination of CERT Organizations in Virginia." Quick Response Report 170, Natural Hazards Center, University of Colorado, Boulder.

Fritz, Charles and Harry B. Williams. 1957a. "The Human Being in Disasters: a Research Perspective." *The Annals of the American Academy of Political and Social Science 309*: 42–51.

Fritz, Charles E. and J.H. Mathewson. 1957b. *Convergence Behavior: a Disaster Control Problem.* Special Report prepared for the Committee on Disaster Studies, National Academy of Sciences, National Research Council.

Fritz, Charles E. and J.H. Mathewson. 1957c. *Convergence Behavior in Disasters: a problem in social control.* Washington D.C.: National Academy of Science, Committee on Disaster Studies, National Research Council Publication #476.

Geertz, Clifford. 1973. *The Interpretation of Cultures.* NY: Basic Books.

Glaser, Barney G. and Anselm L. Strauss. 1965. *Awareness of Dying.* Piscataway, NJ: Transaction Publishers.

Glaser, Barney G. and Anselm L. Strauss. 1967. *The Discovery of Grounded Theory.* NY: Aldine.

Glaser, Barney G. 1992. *Basics of Grounded Theory: emergence vs. forcing.* Mill Valley, CA: The Sociology Press.

Grady, John. 1996. "The Scope of Visual Sociology." *Visual Sociology 11/2:* 10–24.

Golden-Biddle, Karen and Karen Locke. 2007. *Composing Qualitative Research,* second edition. Newbury Park, CA: Sage.

Goffman, Erving. 1959. *The Presentation of Self in Everyday Life.* NY: Doubleday.

Goffman, Erving. 1963. *Behavior in Public Places.* NY: Free Press.

Goffman, Erving. 1979. *Gender Advertisements.* NY: Harper and Row.

Golden-Biddle, Karen and Karen Locke. 2006. *Composing Qualitative Research.* Thousand Oaks, CA: Sage.

Goode, Erich. 1996. "The Ethics of Deception in Social Research: a Case Study." *Qualitative Sociology 19/1:* 11–33.

Gorden, Raymond. 1992. *Basic Interviewing Skills.* Itasca, IL: Peacock Publishers.

Gottdiener, M. 1979. "Field Research and VideoTape." *Sociological Inquiry 49:* 59–63.

Greater New Orleans Community Data Center. 2010. New Orleans Index Five Years Later. New Orleans LA: GNOCDC/Brookings Institution.

Guba, Egon. 1993. "Preface." In Erlandson, David A. et al. 1993. *Doing Naturalistic Inquiry: a guide to methods.* Newbury Park, CA: Sage.

Harper, Douglas. 2002. "Talking about Pictures: a Case for Photo Elicitation." *Visual Studies 17/2:* 13–98.

Harper, Douglas. 1998. "An Argument for Visual Sociology." In: Prosser, Jon (Ed.), Image-based Research: a sourcebook for qualitative researchers."

Herbert, Robin et al. 2006. "The World Trade Center Disaster and the Health of Workers: five-year assessment of a unique medical screening program." *Environmental Health Perspectives 114/12:* 1853–1858.

Hesse-Biber, Sharlene and Patricia Leavy. 2013. *Feminist Research Practice.* Thousand Oaks, CA: Sage.

Hill, Michael R. 1993. *Archival Strategies and Techniques.* Newbury Park, CA: Sage.

Hinshaw, Robert. E. 2006. *Living with Nature's Extremes: The Life of Gilbert Fowler White.* Boulder, Colorado: Johnson Books.

Hyrapiet, Shireen. 2006. *Emergent Phenomena after the Indian Ocean Tsunami.* Stillwater, OK: Thesis, Fire and Emergency Management Program.

Hockings, Paul, Ed. 1995. *Principles of Visual Anthropology.* NY: Mouton de Gruyter.

Hoffman, Susanna and Anthony Oliver-Smith, Eds. 2002. *Catastrophe and Culture.* Santa Fe: School of American Research Press.

Hovey, Wendy. 2007. "Examining the Role of Social Media in Organization-Volunteer Relationships." *Public Relations Journal.* 4.

Irvine, Leslie. 2004. "Providing for Pets During Disasters: an Exploratory Study." Quick Response Research Report #171. University of Colorado: Natural Hazards Center.

Irvine, Leslie. 2006. "Providing for Pets during Disasters, Part II: Animal Response Volunteers in Gonzales, Louisiana." Quick Response Report #187, Natural Hazards Center, University of Colorado.

Irvine, Leslie. 2009. *Filling the Ark: Animal Welfare in Disasters.* Philadelphia: Temple University Press.

Jenkins, Pam and Brenda D. Phillips. 2008. "Battered Women, Catastrophe and the Context of Safety." *NWSA Journal 20/3*: 49–68.

Johnson, Norris R. 1988. "Fire in a Crowded Theater." *International Journal of Mass Emergencies and Disasters 6/1*: 7–26.

Johnson, Norris R. 1987. "Panic at the Who Concert Stampede." *Social Problems 34/4*: 362–378.

Jones, James. 1981. *Bad Blood: the Tuskegee Syphilis Experiment.* NY: The Free Press.

Kendra, James and Tricia Wachtendorf. 2001. "Rebel Food...Renegade Supplies: Convergence after the World Trade Center Attack." Newark, DE: University of Delaware, Disaster Research Center.

Kendra, James and Tricia Wachtendorf. 2006. "Community Innovation and Disasters." In: Rodríguez, Havidán, Enrico L. Quarantelli and Russell R. Dynes, (Eds.), *Handbook of Disaster Research*, 316–334. NY: Springer.

Killian, Lewis M. 2002. "An Introduction to Methodological Problems of Field Studies in Disasters." In: *Methods of Disaster Research*, Robert A. Stallings (Ed.), 49–93. Philadelphia, PA: Xlibris/International Research Committee on Disasters.

Kreps, Gary and Susan Bosworth. 1994. *Organizing, Role Enactment, and Disaster.* Cranbury, NJ: Associated University Presses, Inc.

Kreps, Gary and Susan Lovegren Bosworth. 2006. "Organizational Adaptation to Disaster." In: Rodríguez, Havidán, Enrico L. Quarantelli and Russell R. Dynes, (Eds.), *Handbook of Disaster Research*, 297–315. NY: Springer.

Krueger, Richard A. and Mary Anne Casey. 2000. *Focus Groups.* Newbury Park, CA: Sage.

Kunreuther, Howard. 2006. "Disaster Mitigation and Insurance: learning from Katrina." *ANNALS, AAPSS*: 208–227.

Kunreuther, Howard and Richard J. Roth Sr., eds. 1998. *Paying the Price.* Washington D.C.: Joseph Henry Press.

Landrigan Phillip J. et al. 2004. "Health and Environmental Consequences of the World Trade Center Disaster." *Environmental Health Perspectives 112/6*: 731–739.

Letukas, Lynn and John Barnshaw. 2008. "A World System View to Post-Catastrophe International Relief." *Social Forces 87/2*: 1063–1087.

Lincoln, Yvonna and Egon Guba. 1985. *Naturalistic Inquiry.* Newbury Park, CA: Sage.

Lofland, John, David Snow, Leon Anderson and Lyn H. Lofland. 2006. *Analyzing Social Settings*, 4th edition. Belmont, CA: Wadsworth.

Lois, Jennifer. 2003. *Heroic Efforts: The Emotional Culture of Search and Rescue Volunteers*. NY: New York University Press.

Lowe, Setha, and Alice Fothergill. 2003. "A Need to Help: Emergent Volunteer Behavior after September 11th." In: J. Monday, (Ed.), *Beyond September 11th: An Account of Post*-disaster Research, 293–314. Boulder, CO: Natural Hazards Research and Applications Information Center.

MacDonal, Elspeth, Theresia Citraningtyas, and Beverly Raphael. 2012. "Disaster Experiences in the Context of Life: Perspectives Five to Six Years after the 2003 Canberra Bushfire." *Journal of Emergency Primary Health Care 8/2*: 1–9.

Marshall, Catherine and Gretchen B. Rossman. 1998. *Designing Qualitative Research*, 3rd edition. Thousand Oaks, CA: Sage.

McEntire, David. 2004. "The Status of Emergency Management Theory: Issues, Barriers, and Recommendations for Improvement." Presented at the FEMA Higher Education Conference June 8, 2004, Emmitsburg, MD.

McEntire, David A., Robie J. Robinson, Richard T. Weber. 2003. "Business Responses to the World Trade Center Disaster: a study of corporate roles, functions, and interaction with the public sector." In: Jacquelyn Monday (Ed.), *Beyond September 11th*, 431–455. Boulder, CO: University of Colorado, Natural Hazards Center.

Michaels, Sarah. 2003. "Perishable Information, Enduring Insights, Understanding Quick Response Research." J. Monday (Ed.), *Beyond September 11th: an account of post-disaster research*, 15–48. Boulder, CO: University of Colorado Natural Hazards Center.

Mileti, Dennis. 1999. *Disasters by Design*. Washington D.C.: Joseph Henry Press.

Milgram, Stanley. 1974. *Obedience to Authority: an Experimental View*. NY: Harper Collins.

Mileti, Dennis, Thomas Drabek, and Eugene Haas. 1975. *Human Systems in Extreme Environments: a Sociological Perspective*. Boulder, CO: The University of Colorado, Institute of Behavioral Science Monograph #21.

Mileti, Dennis et al. 1995. "Toward an Integration of Natural Hazards and Sustainability." *Environmental Professional 17*(2): 117–126.

Mitchell, James K. 2008. "Including the Capacity for Coping with Surprises in Post-disaster Recovery Policies. Reflections on the experience of Tangshan, China." *Behemoth*: Vol. 1, No. 03, pp. 21–38.

Mitchell, Terry, Kara Griffin, Sherry H. Stewart, and Pamela Lofa. 2004. "We Will Never Forget: The Swissair Flight 111 Disaster and Its Impact on Volunteers and Communities." *Journal of Health Psychology 9/2*: 245–262.

Monday, Jacquelyn, ed. 2003. *Beyond September 11th*. Boulder, CO: University of Colorado, Natural Hazards Center.

Musick, Marc, John Wilson and William B. Bynum, Jr. 2000. "Race and Formal Volunteering: the differential effects of class and religion." *Social Forces 78/4*: 1539–1571.

Musson, R.M.W. 1986. "The Use of Newspaper Data in Historical Earthquake Studies." *Disasters 10*: 217–223.

Neal, David M., 2003. "Design Characteristics of Emergency Operating Centers." *Journal of Emergency Management* 1/2: 35–38.

Newman, Elana and Danny G. Kaloupek. 2004. "The Risks and Benefits of Participating in Trauma-Focused Research Studies." *Journal of Traumatic Stress* 17/5: 383–394.

National Academies. 2012. *Disaster Resilience*. Washington D.C.: National Academies.

National Council on Disability. 2009. *Effective Emergency Management*. Washington D.C.: National Council on Disability.

National Governor's Association. 1979. *Comprehensive Emergency Management*. Washington D.C.: National Governor's Association.

National Organization on Disability. 2005. *Special Needs Assessment of Katrina Evacuees (S.N.A.K.E. Report)*. Washington D.C.: National Organization on Disability.

National Voluntary Organizations Active in Disaster. No date. *Managing spontaneous volunteers in times of disaster: the synergy of structure and good intentions*. http://1www.nvoad.org/library/cat_view/11-volunteer-management, last accessed September 30, 2013. Accessed January 15, 2008.

Neal, David M. 1990. "Volunteer Organizations following the Loma Prieta Earthquake: A Look at Tasks, Organizational Networks, and Effectiveness." In. Bolin, Robert (Ed.), *Response to the Loma Prieta Earthquake*, 91–97. Boulder, Colorado, Institute of Behavioral Sciences.

Neal, David M., 2003. "Design Characteristics of Emergency Operating Centers." *Journal of Emergency Management* 1.2: 35–38.

Neal, David M., 2004. "Transition from Response to Recovery after the Lancaster, Texas, Tornado: An Empirical Description." *Journal of Emergency Management* 2/1: 47–51.

Neal, David M., 2005. "Case Studies of Four Emergency Operating Centers," *Journal of Emergency Management* 3/1: 29–32.

Neal, David M., 2013. "Disaster and Social Time." *International Journal of Mass Emergencies and Disaster* 31(1): 247–270.

Neal, David M., and Gary Webb. 2006. "Structural Barriers to Implementing the National Incident Management System." In: Bevc, Christine, Learning from Catastrophe: Quick Response Research in the Wake of *Hurricane Katrina*, 263–284. Boulder, CO: Natural Hazards Center, University of Colorado.

Nepal, Vishnu, Deborah Banerjee, Monica Slentz, Frank Perry and Deborah Scott. 2010. "Community-Based Participatory Research in Disaster Preparedness among Linguistically Isolated Populations: A Public Health Perspective." *Journal of Empirical Research on Human Research Ethics: An International Journal* 5(4): 53–63.

Newman, Elana and Danny G. Kaloupek. 2004. "The Risks and Benefits of Participating in Trauma-Focused Research Studies." *Journal of Traumatic Stress* 17/5: 383–394.

Nigg, Joanne, John Barnshaw, and Manuel R. Torres. 2006. "Hurricane Katrina and the Flooding of New Orleans: Emergent Issues in Sheltering and Temporary Housing." *The Annals of the American Academy of Political and Social Science* 604/1: 113–128.

Norris, Fran. H., M. J. Friedman, P. J. Watson, C. M. Byrne, E. Diaz, and K. Kaniasty. 2002b. "60,000 Disaster Victims Speak: Part I. An Empirical Review of the Empirical Literature, 1981–2001." *Psychiatry* 65 (3):207–239.

Norris, Fran. H., M. J. Friedman, and P. J. Watson. 2002a. "60,000 Disaster Victims Speak: Part II. Summary and Implications of the Disaster Mental Health Research." *Psychiatry* 65 (3):240–260.

North, Carol et. Al. 2002. "Coping, Functioning, and Adjustment of Rescue Workers after the Oklahoma City Bombing." *Journal of Traumatic Stress* 15 (3):171–175.

NVOAD/National Voluntary Organizations Active in Disaster. No date. *Managing Spontaneous Volunteers.* Available at http://www.nvoad.org/library/cat_view/11-volunteer-management, last accessed March 31, 2013.

Oklahoma Mesonet. 2012. "Oklahoma's Drought Continues to Expand." Available at http://www.mesonet.org/index.php/news/article/oklahoma_drought_continues_to_expand, last accessed January 28, 2013.

Oliver-Smith, Anthony. 1986. *The Martyred City: Death and Rebirth in the Andes.* Albuquerque: University of New Mexico Press.

Oliver-Smith, Anthony, Ed. 2009. *Development and Dispossession.* Santa Fe: School for Advanced Research Press.

Olson, R. et al. 1998. "Night and Day: mitigation policymaking in Oakland, California before and after the Loma Prieta earthquake." *International Journal of Mass Emergencies and Disasters* 16: 145–179.

OXFAM. (No date) "The tsunami's impact on women." OXFAM briefing Note, OXFAM International.

Palen, L., A. Hughes. 2009. Twitter Adoption and Use in Mass Convergence and Emergency Events.*6th International ISCRAM Conference,* Gothenburg, Sweden.

Paton, Douglas, et al. 2008. "Living with Bushfire Risk: Social and Environmental Influences on Preparedness." *The Australian Journal of Emergency Management* 23/3: 41–48.

Peacock, Walter, Betty H. Morrow, and Hugh Gladwin. 1997. *Hurricane Andrew.* London: Routledge.

Peek, Lori. 2003. "Reactions and Response: Muslim Students' Experienceson New York City Campuses Post 9/11." *Journal of Muslim Minority Affairs* 23/2: 273–285.

Peek, Lori. 2011. *Behind the Backlash: Muslim Americans after 9/11.* Philadelphia: Temple University Press.

Peek, Lori and Lynn Weber, eds. 2013. *Displaced: Life in the Katrina Diaspora.* Austin, TX: University of Texas Press.

Peek, Lori and Alice Fothergill. 2009. "Using Focus Groups: from Studying Daycare centers, 9/11, and Hurricane Katrina." *Qualitative Research* 9/1: 31–59.

Peek, Lori, Jeanette Sutton, J. Gump J. 2008. "Caring for Children in the Aftermath of Disaster: the Church of the Brethren Children's Disaster Services Program." *Children, Youth and Environments* 18: 408–421.

Perry, Ronald W. 2006. "What is a Disaster?" In: Rodríguez, Havidán, Enrico L. Quarantelli and Russell R. Dynes (Eds.), *Handbook of Disaster Research,* 1–15. NY: Springer.

Perry, Ron and Mike Lindell. 1997. "Principles for Managing Community Relocation as a Hazard Mitigation Measure." *Journal of Contingencies and Crisis Management* 5/1: 125–145.

Perry, Ronald W. and E.L. Quarantelli, Eds. 2005. *What is a Disaster? New Answers on the Question.* International Research Committee on Disasters: Xlibris.

Pfefferbaum, B., J. A. Call, and G. M. Sconzo. 1999. "Mental Health Services for Children in the First Two Years after the 1995 Oklahoma City Terrorist Bombing." *Psychiatric Services 50/7*: 956–958.

Pike, Lynn, Brenda Phillips and Patsilu Reeves. 2006. "Shelter life after Katrina: a Visual Analysis of Evacuee Perspectives." *International Journal of Mass Emergencies and Disasters 24/3*: 303–330.

Phillips, Brenda D. 1997. "Qualitative Disaster Research." *International Journal of Mass Emergencies and Disasters 15/1*: 179–195.

Phillips, Brenda D. 2010. *Disaster Recovery.* Boca Raton, FL: CRC Press.

Phillips, Brenda D. 2013. Mennonite Disaster Service: Building a Therapeutic Community after the U.S. Gulf Coast Storms. Lanham, MD: Lexington Books.

Phillips, Brenda and Pam Jenkins. 2010. "Violence and Disaster Vulnerability." In: Phillips, Brenda, Deborah S.K. Thomas, Alice Fothergill and Lynn Pike (Eds.), *Social Vulnerability to Disasters*, 279–306. Boca Raton, FL: CRC Press.

Phillips, Brenda, Patricia Stukes and Pam Jenkins. 2012. "Freedom Hill is Not for Sale and Neither Is the Lower Ninth Ward." *Journal of Black Studies* 43(4): 405–426.

Phillips, Brenda, Tom Wikle, Angela Head Hakim, Lynn Pike. 2012. "Establishing and Operating Shelters after Hurricane Katrina." *International Journal of Emergency Management.*

Phillips, Brenda, Dave Neal, Tom Wikle, Aswin Subanthore and Shireen Hyrapiet. 2008. "Mass Fatality Management after the Indian Ocean Tsunami." *Disaster Prevention and Management 17/5*: 681–697.

Phillips, Brenda D., Lisa Garza and David M. Neal. 1994. "Intergroup Relations in Disasters: service delivery barriers after Hurricane Andrew." *Journal of Intergroup Relations 21*: 18–27.

Phillips, Brenda, Deborah S.K. Thomas, Alice Fothergill, Lynn Blinn Pike. 2010. *Social Vulnerability to Disasters.* Boca Raton, FL: CRC Press.

Plotkin, Mark J. 1993. *Tales of a Shaman's Apprentice.* NY: Penguin Books.

Plummer, Ken. 2001. *Documents of Life/Documents of Life 2: an invitation to critical humanism.* London: George, Allen, and Unwin.

Prince, Samuel Henry. 1920. *Catastrophe and Social Change.* NY: Columbia University (Monograph).

Quarantelli, E.L. 1982a. *Sheltering and Housing after Major Community Disasters: Case Studies and General Observations.* Newark, DE: Disaster Research Center, University of Delaware.

Quarantelli, E.L. 1982b. "General and Particular Observations on Sheltering and Housing in American Disasters." *Disasters 6/4*: 277–281.

Quarantelli, E.L. Circa 1981. "Class Lecture on Inductive and Deductive Approaches, Qualitative Methods." Columbus, OH: Department of Sociology, The Ohio State University.

Quarantelli, E.L. 1985. *Emergent Citizen Groups in Disaster Preparedness and Recovery Activities.* Final Report, Federal Emergency Management Agency.

Quarantelli, E.L. 1987a. "Disaster studies: an analysis of the social historical factors affecting the development of research in the area." *International Journal of Mass Emergencies and Disasters* 5(3): 285–310.

Quarantelli, E.L. 1987b. "Research in the Disaster Area: What is being done and what should be done?" University of Delaware, Disaster Research Center, Preliminary Paper #118.

Quarantelli, E.L. 1988. "The NORC Research on the Arkansas Tornado: a Fountainhead Study." *International Journal of Mass Emergencies and Disasters* 6(3): 283–310.

Quarantelli, E.L. 1999. *What is a Disaster?* London: Routledge.

Quarantelli, E.L. 1997. "Ten Criteria for Evaluating the Management of Community Disasters." *Disasters* 21(1): 39–56.

Quarantelli, E.L. 2002. "The Disaster Research Center (DRC) Field Studies of Organized Behavior in the Crisis Time Period of Disasters." In: Stallings, Robert (Ed.), *Methods of Disaster Research*, 94–126. Philadelphia: Xlibris/International Research Committee on Disasters.

Quarantelli, E.L. 2005. "Catastrophes Are Different from Disasters." http://understandingkatrina.ssrc.org/Quarantelli/, last accessed January 31, 2013.

Rayner, Jeanette F. 1957. "Studies of Disasters and Other Extreme Situations." *Human Organization* 16/2: 30–40.

Reinharz, Shulamit. 1992. *Feminist Methodology in Social Research.* NY: Oxford.

Richards, Lyn. 1999. *Using NVivo in Qualitative Research.* Newbury Park, CA: Sage.

Richards, Lyn. 2009. *Handling Qualitative Data: a Practical Guide*, 2nd edition. Newbury Park, CA: Sage.

Richardson, Laurel. 1990. *Writing Strategies.* Newbury Park, CA: Sage.

Richardson, Laurel. 1987. *The New Other Woman.* NY: Macmillan.

Roberts, H., Curtis, K. Liabo, D. Rowland, C. DiGiuseppi, I. Roberts. 2004. "Putting Public Health Evidence into Practice." *Journal of Epidemiology and Community Health* 58: 280–5.

Rose, Gillian. 2007. *Visual Methodologies*, 2nd edition. Thousand Oaks, CA: Sage.

Rubin, Herbert J. and Irene S. Rubin. 2012. *Qualitative Interviewing.* Newbury Park, CA: Sage.

Rodriguez, H., J. Trainor and E. L. Quarantelli. 2006. "Rising to the Challenges of a Catastrophe." *Annals of the American Academy of Political and Social Science* 604: 82–101.

Rosenstein, Donald L. 2004. "Decision-Making Capacity and Disaster Research." *Journal of Traumatic Stress* 17/5: 373–381.

Rotanz, Richard. 2006. "From Research to Praxis: the Relevance of Disaster Research for Emergency Management." In: Rodríguez, Havidán, Enrico L. Quarantelli and Russell R. Dynes (Eds.), *Handbook of Disaster Research*, 468–475. NY: Springer.

Saldaña, Johnny. 2003. *Longitudinal Qualitative Research.* Walnut Creek, CA: AltaMira Press.

Scanlon, T. Joseph. 2002. "Rewriting a Living Legend: Researching the 1917 Halifax Explosion." In: Stallings Robert, *Methods of Disaster Research*, 266–301. Philadelphia, PA: Xlibris/International Research Committee on Disasters.

Scanlon, T. Joseph. 2006. "Dealing with the Tsunami Dead." *Australian Journal of Emergency Management 21*/2: 57–61.

Schatzman, Leonard and Anselm Strauss. 1973. *Field Research*. Englewood Cliffs NJ: Prentice Hall.

Sharkey Peter. 2007. "Survival and Death in New Orleans: an empirical look at the human impact of Katrina." *Journal of Black Studies 37*/4: 482–501.

Shaw, Rajib. And Katsuihciro Goda. 2004. "From Disaster to Sustainable Civil Society: the Kobe experience." *Disasters 28*/1: 16–40.

Silverman, David. 2000. *Doing Qualitative Research: a Practical Handbook*. Newbury Park, CA: Sage.

Simpson, David and Steven Stehr. 2003. "Victim Management and Identification after the World Trade Center Collapse." In: Jacquelyn Monday (Ed.), Beyond September 11th, 109–119. Boulder, CO: University of Colorado, Natural Hazards Center.

Snow, David A. and Leon Anderson. 1993. *Down on their Luck: A Study of Homeless Street People*. Berkeley, CA: University of California Press.

Stallings, Robert A., Ed. 2002. *Methods of Disaster Research*. Philadelphia, PA: Xlibris/International Research Committee on Disasters.

Stallings, Robert A. 2006. "Methodological Issues." In: Rodríguez, Havidán, Enrico L. Quarantelli and Russell R. Dynes (Eds.), *Handbook of Disaster Research*, 55–82. NY: Springer.

Solis, Gabriela, Henry Hightower, June Kawaguchi. 1995. *Disaster Debris Management*. Vancouver: University of British Columbia, Disaster Preparedness Resources Centre.

Spradley, James P. 1979. *The Ethnographic Interview*. NY: Holt.

Spradley, James P. 1980. *Participant Observation*. NY: Holt, Rinehart and Winston.

Stasz, Clarice. 1979. "The Early History of Visual Sociology." In: *Images of Information*, Jon Wagner (Ed.), 119–135. Beverly Hills, CA: Sage.

Strauss, Anselm and Juliet Corbin. 1993. *Basics of Qualitative Research: Grounded Theory Techniques*. Newbury Park, CA: Sage.

Sjoberg, Misa, Claes Wallenius and Gerry Larsson. 2006. "Leadership in Complex, Stressful, Rescue Operations: a qualitative study." *Disaster Prevention and Management 15*/4: 576–584.

Stallings, Robert A., and E. L. Quarantelli. 1985. "Emergent Citizen Groups and Emergency Management." *Public Administration Review*. 45: 93–100.

Stokes, Donald. 1997. *Pasteur's Quadrant: Basic Science and Technological Innovation*. Washington D.C.: Brookings Institution.

Stough, Laura and Sharp, Amy. 2008. *"An Evaluation of the National Disability Rights Network Participation in the Katrina Aid Today Project."* Washington, D.C.: The National Disability Rights Network.

Stough, Laura M., Amy N. Sharp, Curt Decker, and Nachama Walker. 2010. "Disaster Case Management and Individuals with Disabilities." *Rehabilitation Psychology 55*/3: 211–220.

Sutton, Jeanette. 2003. "A Complex Organizational Adaptation to the World Trade Center Disaster: an Analysis of Faith-based Organizations." In: Monday, J. (Ed.). *Beyond September 11th: an account of post-disaster research*, 405–428. Boulder, CO: Natural Hazards Applications and Information Research Center.

Sutton Jeanette., Lydia. Palen and Irina Shklovski. 2008. Backchannels on the Front Lines: Emergent Uses of Social Media in the 2007 Southern California Wildfires. Paper presented at the *5th International ISCRAM Conference*, Washington D.C.

Sutton, Jeanette, Brett Hansard and Paul Hewett. 2011. "Changing Channels: communicating tsunami warning information in Hawaii." At http://jeannettesutton.com/uploads/Changing_Channels_FINAL_7-5-11.pdf, last accessed September 30, 2013.

Tatsuki, Shigeo. 1998. "The Kobe Earthquake and the Renaissance of Volunteerism in Japan." Presented at the International Associateion of Volunteer Efforts World Conference. University of Alberta, Edmonton, Canada.

Taylor, Verta. 1977. "Good News About Disaster." *Psychology Today*. October *1977*: 93–98.

Thomas, W.I. and Florian Znaniecki. 1919. *The Polish Peasant in Europe and America*. Chicago, IL: University of Chicago Press.

Thomas, W.I. and Dorothy Swaine Thomas. 1928. *The Child in America*. NY: Knopf.

Thompson, Kenrick S. and Clarke, Alfred C. 1974. "Photographic Imagery and the Viet Nam War: an Unexamined Perspective." *The Journal of Psychology* 87: 279–92.

Thompson, Kenrick S., Alfred C. Clarke and Simon Dinitz. "Reactions to My-Lai: a Visual-Verbal Comparison." *Sociology and Social Research* 58: 122–29 (1974).

Tierney, Kathleen, Michael K. Lindell and Ronald W. Pery. 2001. *Facing the Unexpected*. Washington D.C.: Joseph Henry Press.

Toscani, Letizia. 1998. "Women's Roles in Natural Disaster Preparation and Aid: a Central American View." In: by Enarson, Elaine and Betty Hearn Morrow, (Eds.), *The Gendered Terrain of Disaster: Through Women's Eyes*, 207–212. Miami, FL: Florida International University.

Townsend-Bell, Erica. 2009. "Being True and Being You: race, gender, class and the fieldwork experience." *PS: Political Science and Politics* 42: 311–314.

Tuason, Ma. Teresa G., C. Dominik Güss, and Lynne Carroll. 2012. "The Disaster Continues: a Qualitative Study on the Experiences of Displaced Hurricane Katrina survivors." *Professional Psychology: Research and Practice* 43(4): 288–297.

USAID. 2012. "Fast Facts on the U.S. Government's Work in Haiti: shelter and housing." Available at http://haiti.usaid.gov/issues/shelter.php, last accessed February 12, 2013.

Wagner, Jon, Ed. 1979. *Images of Information*. Newbury Park, CA: Sage.

Wagner-Pacifici, Robin and Barry Schwartz. 1991. "The Vietnam Veterans Memorial: commemorating a difficult past." *American Journal of Sociology* 97: 376–420.

Webb, Eugene et al. 1981. *Nonreactive Measures in the Social Sciences*, 2nd edition. NY: Houghton Mifflin.

Webb, Gary. 2004. "Role Improvising During Crisis Situations." *International Journal of Emergency Management 2/*1: 47–61.

Weber, Lynn, and Lori Peek. 2012. *Displaced: Life in the Katrina Diaspora.* Austin: University of Texas Press.

Whittaker, Joshua, and John Handmer. 2010. "Community Bushfire Safety: a Review of post-Black Saturday Research." *Australian Journal of Emergency Management 26/*4: 7–13.

Williams, Terry et al. 1992. "Personal Safety in Dangerous Places." *Journal of Contemporary Ethnography 21*: 343–374.

Wilson, John. 2000. "Volunteering." *Annual Review of Sociology 26*: 215–240.

Wolcott, Harry F. 2008. *Writing Up Qualitative Research.* Newbury Park, CA: Sage.

Worth, Sol and John Adair. 1970. *Through Navajo Eyes: an Exploration in Film Communication and Anthropology.* Bloomington: Indiana University Press.

Weiss, Robert S. 1994. *Learning from Strangers: the Art and Method of Qualitative Interview Studies.* New York: Macmillan.

Whyte, William Foote. 1955. *Street Corner Society.* Chicago: University of Chicago Press.

Wolcott, Harry F. 1995. *The Art of Fieldwork.* Newbury Park, CA: Sage.

Yin, Robert. 2008. *Case Study Research.* Newbury Park, CA: Sage.

INDEX

Page numbers followed by t or f indicate a table or figure respectively. Page numbers followed by b indicate a box.

Lightning Source UK Ltd.
Milton Keynes UK
UKOW04f1819310315

248870UK00001B/44/P

9 780199 796175